PREACH
FOR A
YEAR #5

Books by Roger Campbell

Preach for a Year #1
Preach for a Year #2
Preach for a Year #3
Preach for a Year #4
Preach for a Year #5
Staying Positive in a Negative World
Weight! A Better Way to Lose
You Can Win!

PREACH FOR A YEAR #5

104 Sermon Outlines

Two complete outlines for every Sunday of the year

Roger Campbell

kregel
PUBLICATIONS

Grand Rapids, MI 49501

Preach for a Year #5 by Roger F. Campbell

Copyright © 1999 by Kregel Publications, a division of Kregel, Inc., P.O. Box 2607, Grand Rapids, MI 49501. Kregel Publications provides trusted, biblical publications for Christian growth and service. Your comments and suggestions are valued.

For more information about Kregel Publications, visit our web site at: www.kregel.com

Cover design: Don Ellens

Library of Congress Cataloging-in-Publication Data
Campbell, Roger F., 1930–
    Preach for a year #5 / by Roger F. Campbell.
        p.   cm.
        1. Sermons—Outlines, syllabi, etc. I. Title.
    BV4223.C33   1999   251'.02—dc20   87-29400
                                                            CIP

ISBN 0-8254-2329-5 (vol. 1)
ISBN 0-8254-2330-9 (vol. 2)
ISBN 0-8254-2321-x (vol. 3)
ISBN 0-8254-2318-x (vol. 4)
ISBN 0-8254-2347-3 (vol. 5)

2 3 4 5 / 03 02 01

Printed in the United States of America

To the Reverend Terry Walker, my pastor and friend, who has arrived in heaven before me.

CONTENTS

CONTENTS 9

INTRODUCTION

When I met Terry Walker, he was a visitor in the Sunday school class for couples I taught at the church where I had recently become the pastor. At that time, Terry conducted an effective greater-Detroit-area youth ministry and had directed youth work in other states preceding his return home. That first Sunday, Terry was just another face in the class. Who would have thought that he would someday become my pastor?

More than twenty years after Terry Walker visited my Sunday school class, my wife, Pauline, and I visited the church where he was the pastor. It didn't take long for me to see why this congregation had grown from a handful to hundreds. Although the talented church staff had played an important role, the preaching of Pastor Terry Walker was the key to this growth.

Why has Pastor Terry's preaching been so effective? I believe there are four basic reasons: his heart for people, his human touch, his sense of humor, and his continual searching of the Scriptures to develop an ever-deepening walk with his Lord.

People found their way to Pastor Terry's church because they would be accepted, loved, and met on common ground. They knew that no matter how tough the week had been, this pastor would have some faith-building human experience to share that would allow them to laugh again. But, most of all, they knew that they were coming to hear a man who knew he could not communicate God's truth unless he lived it every day.

This week, Pastor Terry departed for heaven. That's why I've dedicated *Preach for a Year #5* to his memory. I urge you to preach these sermons with the heartfelt love for people and the Lord that he demonstrated every week. In these difficult days, we need all of that kind of preaching we can get.

ROGER CAMPBELL

11

Evangelism: Watchword for the Year

2 Timothy 4:5

I. **Introduction**
   A. *"Evangelism": What a Good Word!*
      1. It speaks of obeying the Great Commission (Matt. 28:18–20)
      2. It speaks of snatching sinners from hell
      3. It speaks of growing churches
   B. *Evangelism Demands Work*
      1. How should it involve every member of the church?
      2. How does it call for ending spectator Christianity?
      3. How can we do the work of evangelism?

II. **Body**
   A. *Let's Preach the Gospel*
      1. What is the gospel? (1 Cor. 15:3–4)
         a. Christ died for our sins according to the Scriptures
         b. Christ was buried and rose again according to the Scriptures
      2. There is nothing better than the gospel
         a. The gospel is better than social action
         b. The gospel is better than political involvement
         c. The gospel is better than religious ritual
      3. We must preach by our lives and our lips
      4. We must preach from the pulpit and our places of work
      5. We must preach by our witness and our walk
   B. *Let's Plead with Sinners*
      1. Have we forgotten that sinners go to hell?
      2. Do we care? God does (2 Peter 3:9)
         a. The cross says, "God cares about sinners going to hell"
         b. This urgent message must have priority again
   C. *Let's Perfect the Saints (Eph. 4:12)*
      1. Let the saints be perfected by evangelists, pastors, and teachers
      2. Why perfect the saints?

       a. To do the work of the ministry
       b. To motivate them to soul winning
       c. To equip them to disciple new converts
  D. *Let's Pull the Net*
    1. All believers are to be fishers of men (Matt. 4:19)
       a. Fishermen must expect to catch fish
       b. We must give people the opportunity to accept Christ
    2. How shall we pull the net?
       a. Pull the net carefully and prayerfully
       b. Pull the net as led by the Holy Spirit
       c. Pull the net repeatedly and expectantly

III. Conclusion
  A. *Evangelism Will Set the Church Afire*
  B. *Evangelism Will Unite Believers*
  C. *Evangelism Will Require a Call to a New Commitment*

Communion and Evangelism

Matthew 26:17–29

I. **Introduction**
   A. *Jesus Celebrates the Last Passover (vv. 17–25)*
      1. Christ celebrates Israel's deliverance from slavery (Exod. 12)
      2. Christ pictured our deliverance from sin by the blood of the Lamb (1 Peter 1:18–19)
      3. Christ, the Lamb of God, became our Passover (1 Cor. 5:7)
   B. *Jesus Celebrates the First Communion*
      1. The last supper became the first communion
         a. He celebrated the last supper with His disciples
         b. We celebrate that same supper today
      2. What does communion have to do with evangelism?

II. **Body**
   A. *The Bread Reminds Us of His Body (v. 26)*
      1. The humble birth at Bethlehem where He took a body (Phil. 2:5–7)
      2. His body is the vehicle of His earthly ministry
         a. He experienced fatigue, hunger, and temptation
         b. He opened His arms to the needy and the lost
      3. His body bruised and bleeding for our redemption (Isa. 53)
         a. The scourging of Jesus (Matt. 27:26)
         b. The cursing, spitting crowd (vv. 29–30)
         c. The crown of thorns, the nails, and the crucifixion (v. 29)
      4. How many sinners have you told of His love this week?
   B. *The Cup Reminds Us of His Blood (vv. 27–28)*
      1. His blood is "the blood of the New Testament" (v. 28)
         a. All Old Testament sacrifices pointed to the cross

          b. The fulfillment of redemption types are observed under the law

    2. His blood provides remission of sins

          a. God loves sinners (Rom. 5:8)

          b. Sinners can be justified by His blood (Rom. 5:9)

    3. His blood cleanses completely (1 John 1:7–9)

    4. His precious blood redeems sinners (1 Peter 1:19)

    5. Let's tell the good news

  C. *The Bread and the Cup Remind Us of the Blessed Hope (v. 29)*

    1. Communion looks forward to the return of Christ

          a. "In my Father's kingdom"

          b. Paul: Communion until He comes (1 Cor. 11:26)

    2. Communion should remind us of the shortness of time

          a. We must win souls while there is time

          b. Today is the day of salvation (2 Cor. 6:2)

    3. Let each Communion service ignite us for evangelism

III. Conclusion

  A. *Three Calls to Evangelism in Every Communion Service*

    1. The bread, the blood, and the blessed hope

    2. The added urgency of the need to win souls

  B. *Will You Tell Someone of Jesus Before Another Communion?*

Come into the Ark

Bible Invitation Series Begins   *Genesis 7:1–7*

I. Introduction
  A. *Introducing the Series: Bible Invitations*
    1. God calls people to Himself
    2. His invitations are found throughout the Bible
  B. *God's Invitations: Calls of Love*
  C. *The First Invitation in the Bible*
    1. The flood was about to begin
    2. "Come thou and all thy house into the ark"

II. Body
  A. *An Invitation to Survive the Flood*
    1. The wickedness of Noah's time (v. 5)
      a. Wicked in their thoughts
      b. Corrupt in their moral decisions
      c. Violence in their dealings with one another
    2. The judgment that follows wickedness (v. 7)
      a. Destruction is determined against the wicked
      b. The wages of sin is death (Rom. 6:23)
    3. The grace that Noah found in the eyes of the Lord (v. 8)
      a. Grace was offered to a man facing judgment
      b. Grace is still offered to sinful people
      c. Grace is the undeserved favor of God
  B. *An Invitation to Take a Step of Faith*
    1. Noah is invited to come into the ark (7:1)
      a. This demanded a step of faith
      b. Noah had built the ark by faith (Heb. 11:7)
      c. Now he must enter it to be saved from the flood
    2. Noah's salvation was by grace through faith
      a. Our salvation is by grace through faith (Eph. 2:8–9)
      b. Noah was saved from the wrath of God in the flood
      c. We are saved from wrath by faith in Christ (John 3:36)

    C. *An Invitation to Noah's Whole Family*
      1. God said, "and all thy house"
      2. God wants entire families to be saved (Acts
         16:30–31)
        a. He wants the circle unbroken
        b. His faithfulness is to all generations (Ps.
           119:90)
      3. Our most important task is to lead our families to
        Christ
        a. This can be difficult
        b. God will give us wisdom and power to do it

III. Conclusion
    A. *How Will We Respond to This Invitation?*
    B. *Will We Accept God's Invitation to Come to Him in
       Faith?*
    C. *What Are We Doing to Ensure That Our Families Are
       Saved?*
      1. The storm is coming
      2. Are all of your loved ones in the ark?

Come with Us

Bible Invitation Series   *Numbers 10:29*

I. Introduction

  A. *An Invitation from Moses*

    1. An invitation to a member of his family

    2. An invitation to go to the Promised Land

  B. *A Fitting Invitation for the Church to Extend*

    1. "Come with us and we will do thee good"

    2. Everyone needs to hear this invitation

II. Body

  A. *Who Gave This Invitation?*

    1. Those who were journeying to a better land

      a. Israel had been delivered from slavery in Egypt

      b. They were headed for the Promised Land

      c. Christians are headed for heaven (John 14:1–3)

    2. The Promised Land was a gift from God

      a. "The Lord said, 'I will give it you'"

      b. It was a future possession of former slaves

    3. Heaven is a prepared gift for God's people

      a. "I go to prepare a place for you" (John 14:3)

      b. Former slaves to sin are now citizens of heaven (Phil. 3:20)

      c. The gift of eternal life includes the gift of heaven (Rom. 6:23)

  B. *Who Got This Invitation?*

    1. This invitation was given to a person Moses loved

      a. He was part of the family

      b. Moses wanted him to share in the blessings ahead

      c. Moses had a plan for him to serve on the journey (v. 31)

    2. This invitation was given to one who would be helped by accepting it

      a. "Come with us and we will do thee good"

      b. Here was an honest desire to do good to another person

    3. God cares about every person we meet

    4. All who accept our invitation to salvation will receive good things
      a. They will travel with us to heaven
      b. They will share in God's blessings to us along the way

C. *Who Guaranteed This Invitation?*
    1. "The Lord hath spoken good concerning Israel"
    2. Moses had received promises for Israel from the Lord
      a. He received them at the burning bush (Exod. 3–4)
      b. Israel's future was as secure as God's promises
    3. The Lord guarantees our offer of salvation
      a. He promises to save all who come to Him (Heb. 7:25)
      b. He promises to keep them all the way (1 John 5:13)

III. Conclusion
  A. *Let Us Extend This Invitation to All We Meet*
  B. *Let All Know That God Loves Them and Longs to Do Them Good*

Come and Be Clean

Isaiah 1:18

I. **Introduction**
   A. *How Strange That God Invites People to Come to Him!*
      1. One would think that we would be knocking on His door
      2. God seeks us before we seek Him (Luke 19:10)
   B. *Isaiah Called to Invite People to Come and Be Clean*
      1. A wonderful invitation
      2. An invitation that is still being extended
   C. *What's This Invitation All About?*

II. **Body**
   A. *An Invitation to Reason at an Unreasonable Time*
      1. "Come now and let us reason together"
      2. Isaiah's nation was in deep trouble
      3. The people had rebelled against the Lord (vv. 2–4)
         a. They chose not to think about God (v. 3)
         b. Sin was rampant; corruption was everywhere (v. 4)
      4. These wayward ones had not responded to chastening (v. 5)
      5. They were a sin-sick people (v. 6)
      6. Crime and violence characterized the age
      7. Rebellion didn't make sense in light of God's blessings
      8. Still, God invited them to come to Him and reason together
      9. What love!
   B. *An Invitation from God at an Ungodly Time*
      1. The source is "saith the Lord"
      2. God called to those who had forsaken Him (v. 4)
         a. People who rejected His way and His Word
         b. People who had grieved and provoked His Holy Spirit
      3. These people reminded Isaiah of Sodom and Gomorrah (vv. 9–10)
         a. A few righteous ones kept them from destruction

      b. Isaiah called them citizens of those wicked cities

    4. Even their feasts were an abomination to the Lord

    5. Nevertheless, God kept inviting them to come and be clean

  C. *An Invitation for Cleansing at a Sinful Time*

    1. This is an invitation to be forgiven

      a. From scarlet red to as white as snow

      b. From crimson red to as white as wool

    2. This was the desire of David's heart after his sin (Ps. 51:7)

      a. "Purge me with hyssop and I shall be clean"

      b. "Wash me and I shall be whiter than snow"

    3. God meets sinners where they are and cleanses them

III. Conclusion

  A. *God Is Still Calling to the Unreasonable and the Ungodly*

  B. *He Will Forgive and Cleanse All Who Come to Him*

  C. *His Blood Still Makes Guilty Ones Clean (1 John 1:9; Rev. 1:5)*

  D. *Isn't It Reasonable to Respond to His Call?*

Come and Be Satisfied

Bible Invitation Series *Isaiah 55:1–2*

I. Introduction

   A. *This Is a Preparation for a Great Invitation (Isa. 54)*
      1. A chapter of comfort and faith
         a. Sing, break forth into singing (v. 1)
         b. Expect greater blessings (vv. 3–4)
         c. Fear not (vv. 4–10)
      2. A chapter guaranteeing protection (vv. 11–17)
   B. *Now We're Prepared for a Life-Changing Invitation*
      1. Come and satisfy your thirst
      2. Come and satisfy your hunger
      3. Come and satisfy your soul

II. Body

   A. *Come and Satisfy Your Thirst (v. 1)*
      1. Thirst is common to all
         a. We all understand this craving
         b. We become especially thirsty in dry times
      2. Thirst speaks of deep inner cravings
      3. Many people make vain attempts to satisfy human thirst
         a. Money, possessions, position, or prestige
         b. Alcohol, other drugs, pleasure, or pride
      4. Our Lord invites us to come and drink living water (John 4)
      5. "Water is, in Isaiah, the common metaphor for divine grace" *(The Pulpit Commentary)*
   B. *Come and Satisfy Your Hunger*
      1. Hunger alerts us to the need for nourishing food
      2. Spiritual hunger calls for the Bread of Life
      3. Blessings are promised to the spiritually hungry (Matt. 5:6)
      4. Human efforts to satisfy spiritual hunger fail
      5. Only Jesus satisfies this inner appetite
   C. *Come and Satisfy Your Soul (v. 2)*
      1. "Let your soul delight in fatness"
      2. People search for satisfaction of soul

        a.   Spending money for that which is not bread
        b.   Laboring for things that do not satisfy
   3.   "Eat that which is good"
        a.   Satisfaction of soul comes through faith in Christ
        b.   All other routes to satisfaction are counterfeits

III. **Conclusion**
   A. *We Are All Invited to a Feast*
      1. Water to quench our thirst
      2. Nourishing food to satisfy our hunger
      3. Spiritual food to satisfy the soul
   B. *We Are All Invited to a Free Feast*
      1. Jesus paid it all
      2. Let all hungry and thirsty ones come to Him and be satisfied

Come and Return to the Lord

Bible Invitation Series   *Hosea 6:1–2*

I. **Introduction**
   A. *The Bible—A Book of Invitations*
      1. The first invitation in the Bible is in Genesis 7:1
      2. The last invitation in the Bible is in Revelation 22:17
      3. Some invitations are from God and others from man
   B. *An Invitation from a Prophet to His People*
      1. Hosea calls his people to return to the Lord
      2. This is a call to personal and national revival
      3. We need a call to revival today
   C. *Considering Hosea's Invitation*

II. **Body**
   A. *An Invitation to Those Who Have Known the Closeness of the Lord*
      1. "Come, let us return"
         a. "Return" reveals that there had been a better time
         b. It was a time of close fellowship with the Lord
      2. Do you remember a better day?
         a. A time when Christ seemed closer than today?
         b. A time when the joy of the Lord was more real?
         c. A time when prayer was more meaningful?
         d. A time when church services were more exciting?
         e. A time when you cared more for souls?
      3. These believers had left their first love for the Lord
         a. Like the church at Ephesus (Rev. 2:1–5)
         b. Like many Christians today
   B. *An Invitation to Those Who Have Felt the Chastening of the Lord*
      1. "He hath torn . . . He hath smitten"
         a. These are harsh words concerning the work of God
         b. Why would God bring trouble to His children?

25

     2. He chastens those He loves (Heb. 12:5–6)
     3. Sin had become a way of life for these people
        (4:1–2)
     4. Are you toying with temptation? Yielding to its
        call?
     5. You are living dangerously; *Return to the Lord!*
  C. *An Invitation to Backsliders to Come Back to the Lord*
     1. "Come . . . He will heal us . . . He will bind us up"
     2. What good news: God loves us in spite of our
        backsliding
        a. He will revive us
        b. He will raise us up
        c. We shall live in His sight
     3. Return to the Lord while you have time to respond
        to His call

III. Conclusion
  A. *Christ Was Torn and Smitten for Us (Isa. 53)*
  B. *Christ Was Raised and Lives to Revive Us*
  C. *Come to Him and He Will Restore Your Soul (Ps. 23)*

Come and Find Rest

Bible Invitation Series   *Matthew 11:28–30*

I. **Introduction**
   A. *Our Inviting Lord*
      1. His invitations are expressions of His love
      2. They are extended to both saints and sinners
   B. *The First Invitation in the New Testament*
      1. An invitation to the weary
      2. An invitation to find rest

II. **Body**
   A. *An Invitation to Physical Rest (v. 28)*
      1. The invitation is to "all ye that labor"
      2. Jesus identifies with working people
         a. He knows about long hours of hard labor
         b. He spoke of sowers, shepherds, fishermen, etc.
         c. He chose hard-working men to be His disciples
      3. Are you tired, wondering how to find strength to go on?
         a. Jesus understands and cares
         b. He offers strength to you (Isa. 40:31; Phil. 4:13)
      4. Those who come to Jesus find rest
         a. They find strength in worship
         b. They are refreshed by resting in Him
   B. *An Invitation to Emotional Rest (v. 28)*
      1. The invitation is to those who "are heavy laden"
      2. Emotional burdens drain our strength
         a. Worry makes us tired
         b. Cares rob us of energy
      3. Those who are heavy laden with cares find rest in Christ, the Problem Solver
         a. We cast our cares on Him (1 Peter 5:7)
         b. He gives peace when we are troubled (John 14:27)
         c. His peace guards our hearts (Phil. 4:6–8)
         d. His grace is sufficient for all our needs (2 Cor. 12:9)

C. *An Invitation to Spiritual Rest (v. 29)*
1. The promise is "ye shall find rest unto your souls"
2. Our souls never rest until they rest in Him
3. Humans struggle for rest of soul
    a. We try works, religious ritual, and the pursuit of perfection
    b. We make efforts to keep the law
    c. These all bring spiritual exhaustion
4. Only Christ brings rest of soul
    a. Note the pronouns of rest (*me, I, my, me, I, my, and my*)
    b. Faith comes not by works or ritual but by faith (Eph. 2:8–9)

III. Conclusion
A. *Come to Jesus, and Find Complete Rest in Him*
B. *Those Yoked with Christ by Faith Enjoy Serving Him*

Let the Children Come

Bible Invitation Series   *Matthew 19:13–15*

I. **Introduction**
   A. *Is Child Evangelism Really Important?*
      1. Children can be noisy in church
      2. Children require special programs
      3. Children don't give much money
   B. *Why, Then, Try to Reach Children?*
      1. The love of God for all (John 3:16)
      2. The cost of the cross (Rom. 5:8)
      3. The invitation of Jesus (vv. 13–15)

II. **Body**
   A. *There Will Always Be Helpers in Reaching Children (v. 13)*
      1. People brought children to Jesus
      2. People are still eager to bring children to Jesus
         a. Loving parents bring children to Jesus
         b. Concerned youth workers bring children to Jesus
         c. Bus drivers and Sunday school teachers bring children to Jesus
      3. Many people in the church show God's love for children
   B. *There Will Always Be Hindrances to Reaching Children (v. 13)*
      1. "The disciples rebuked them" (turned them away)
         a. They thought Jesus was too busy
         b. They thought adults were more important
         c. They underestimated the love of Christ
      2. Many people still overlook the needs of children
      3. These people fail to see the potential in a child
         a. A child has a full life to give to Jesus
         b. Each child is one for whom Christ died
         c. People who are converted as children are the most likely to enter full-time service
      4. People who overlook children are unlike Jesus
   C. *There Will Always Be Hope for All Children (vv. 14–15)*
      1. Jesus had time for the children

      a. He valued them highly
      b. He was not too busy for them
   2. Jesus said, "Forbid them not"
      a. Jesus told the disciples to permit the children to come to Him
      b. No one should forbid children to come to Him
   3. Jesus said, "Of such is the kingdom of heaven"
      a. We must all come to Jesus in childlike faith
      b. Each child should remind us of the simplicity of the gospel
   4. Jesus laid His hands on the children
   5. Jesus prayed for the children

III. Conclusion
   A. *Who Will Come to Jesus with the Faith of a Child?*
   B. *Who Will Take the Time and Effort to Bring Children to Jesus?*

A Challenging Invitation

Bible Invitation Series   *Mark 8:34–37*

I. Introduction

A. *Different Kinds of Invitations*
1. Invitations to salvation
    a. All of us are in need of this invitation (Rom. 3:23)
    b. All of us can accept this invitation (Rom 5:8; 10:9, 13)
2. Invitations to find comfort (Matt. 11:28)
3. Invitations to pray in times of need (Jer. 33:3)

B. *Now a Challenging Invitation*
1. An invitation to discipleship
2. An invitation to count the cost
3. An invitation to suffering, deprivation, and even martyrdom

C. *What This Challenging Invitation Is All About*

II. Body

A. *A Challenge to Forget Self*
1. "Let him deny himself"
2. This is not an easy challenge to accept
    a. We're all prone to look out for number one
    b. Even the disciples longed for high places (Mark 10:27–40)
3. Discipleship calls for giving Christ first place
    a. Seek first the kingdom of God (Matt. 6:33)
    b. Christ has to have the preeminence (Col. 1:17–18)
4. Who's on the throne of your life?
5. Who has first place, self or the Savior?

B. *A Challenge to Full Surrender*
1. "Let him . . . take up his cross"
2. The cross is about death
    a. Jesus had just revealed His coming death (v. 31)
    b. Peter rebelled at this message (v. 32)
    c. He didn't yet understand God's plan of redemption
3. Taking up the cross is about full surrender

   a. Christ surrendered Himself to the cross to save us

   b. We are to surrender to Him in everything

  4. What are you holding back from your Lord?

 C. *A Challenge to Follow Our Savior*

  1. "Let him . . . follow me"

  2. Only the saved can follow Jesus

   a. The indwelling Holy Spirit makes this possible (John 14:17)

   b. He enables us to endure hardship for Christ

  3. Following Christ may lead through difficult places

  4. That's what discipleship is all about

III. **Conclusion**

 A. *Accepting This Challenging Invitation Makes Life Worthwhile*

 B. *In Holding Back, We Lose the Best in Life (v. 35)*

 C. *Will You Accept the Challenges of Discipleship?*

Come and See

Bible Invitation Series   *John 1:35–42*

I. Introduction
  A. *John's Revealing Statement*
     1. "Behold the Lamb of God" (v. 36)
     2. Two of John's disciples leave, following the Lamb
        (v. 37)
  B. *Two Curious Disciples (v. 37–38)*
     1. The Lord's question: "What seek ye?"
     2. Andrew and his friend called Jesus "Rabbi
        (Master)"
     3. They wanted to know where Jesus lived
  C. *The Lord's Invitation to Us All: "Come and See"*

II. Body
  A. *Come and See, and Trust Him Today (vv. 38–39)*
     1. John's statement has pointed the way
        a. They now know that Jesus is the prophesied
           One
        b. This is why they follow Him
        c. This is why they want to know more about
           Him
     2. God always has key people to point others to the
        Lamb of God
        a. Philip and the Ethiopian eunuch (Acts 8:26–40)
        b. Peter and Cornelius (Acts 10)
     3. Who is responsible for you being here today?
     4. See Jesus for who He is (the Savior), and trust Him
        to save you
     5. Like the psalmist, you'll find in Him all you need
        (Ps. 34:8)
  B. *Come and See, and You'll Want to Stay (v. 39)*
     1. "They came . . . and abode with him that day"
     2. How sweet the hours when they were with Jesus!
        a. They didn't want to leave
        b. Every day with Jesus is sweeter than the day
           before
     3. Peter, James, and John were on the Mount of
        Transfiguration (Matt. 17:1–5)

        a. They got a glimpse of the glory of Christ
        b. They just wanted to stay there (v. 4)
    4. You'll wonder why you wasted time in the world
    5. Like Paul, you'll count all things but loss for Christ (Phil. 3)

  C. *Come and See, and You'll Show Others the Way (vv. 40–42)*
    1. Andrew couldn't keep this good news to himself
    2. He went first to find his brother, Simon Peter, to tell him the good news
        a. "We have found the Messiah . . . the Christ"
        b. News like this must be shared
        c. He brought Peter to Jesus
    3. Who brought you to Jesus?
    4. Andrew's first convert would reach thousands of other people for Christ
    5. Be an Andrew; tell others about your Savior

III. Conclusion
  A. *Faith in Christ Must Be Firsthand*
  B. *Jesus Is All You Need*
  C. *Come and See*

Come and Be Safe

Bible Invitation Series   *John 6:37*

I. Introduction
   A. *D. L. Moody's Text*
      1. A text in which he found assurance
      2. A text that made him feel secure
   B. *A Tender Invitation*
      1. Just come to Jesus
      2. He will not cast you out
   C. *Why Believing This Text Brings a Sense of Safety*

II. Body
   A. *To Come to Jesus Is to Receive Him*
      1. "Him that cometh to me. . . ."
      2. There is nothing complicated about this invitation
         a. Nothing about religious ceremony
         b. Nothing about good works
         c. Nothing about giving money
      3. Receiving Christ is placing faith in Him
         a. We become aware of our sinful condition (Rom. 3:10–23)
         b. We understand we cannot save ourselves (Titus 3:5)
         c. We stop trying to earn favor with God (Eph. 2:8–9)
         e. We trust in the Lord Jesus Christ as personal Savior (John 1:12)
      4. We have now come to Jesus
   B. *To Come to Jesus Is to Be Received by Him*
      1. "I will in no wise cast out"
      2. Those who come find Christ's arms open wide to receive them
      3. Here is a two-way meeting:
         a. A seeking sinner meets a seeking Savior
         b. A receiving sinner meets a receiving Savior
      4. The moment we meet we become the children of God (John 1:12)
         a. We become heirs of God, joint heirs with Christ (Rom. 8:17)

35

      b. We will never be separated from His love
        (Rom. 8:38–39)
    5. Every day then becomes an adventure in faith
       (Rom. 1:17; 5:1)
  C. *To Come to Jesus Is to Receive Eternal Life from Him*
    1. "I will in no wise cast out"
      a. A guarantee that bears repeating
      b. A promise that assures eternal life
    2. The verses that follow seal this promise (vv. 38–40)
      a. Christ came to do the Father's will (v. 38)
      b. The Father wills that not one believer be lost
        (v. 39)
      c. The Father wills that all believers be
        resurrected (v. 39)
      d. The Father wills that all believers have
        everlasting life (v. 40)
    3. Those who come to Jesus are safe in His arms

III. **Conclusion**
  A. *Why Would Anyone Delay Coming to Receive Jesus?*
  B. *Come Just as You Are to Receive and Be Received*
     Today

Come to the Mission Field

Bible Invitation Series   *Acts 16:9*

I. **Introduction**
   A. *Exciting Times for the Early Church*
      1. At Pentecost three thousand souls were saved
      2. Believers and churches multiplied
      3. Paul changed from a persecutor to a preacher
      4. He went on missionary journeys to tell the good news
   B. *Paul's Vision at Troas (16:8–10)*
      1. He heard the Macedonian call
      2. "Come over into Macedonia and help us"
   C. *Lessons from Paul's Macedonian Call*

II. **Body**
   A. *Lost Souls Call Us to the Mission Field (v. 9)*
      1. These people are lost in sin and without hope (Eph. 2:12)
      2. These people have never heard the gospel
         a. They do not know that God loves them
         b. They do not know that Christ died to save them
         c. They do not know that He arose and offers them eternal life
      3. How can they believe when they have not heard (Rom. 10:14)?
      4. How can they hear without a preacher (Rom. 10:14)?
         a. Do you hear the calls of the lost?
         b. Are you willing to tell them of Christ and His love?
   B. *Love for Souls Should Cause Us to Heed the Call (vv. 10–40)*
      1. Paul had a deep love for souls
         a. Consider his love for lost Jews (Rom. 9:1–3)
         b. Consider his love for lost Gentiles (missionary journeys)
      2. See how quickly Paul and Silas responded to the call (immediately)

37

3. They went on to Philippi, the chief city of Macedonia
   a. Paul preached at a prayer meeting by a river, and Lydia was converted
   b. He delivered a demon-possessed fortune teller (vv. 16–18)
4. In prison, Paul and Silas reached the jailer for Christ (vv. 23–34)
   a. Their praying and praising God in the prison brought an earthquake
   b. The suicidal jailer became a believer
5. Great victories await us when we heed the call to reach the lost

C. *Look Around! The Mission Field Surrounds Us*
1. The field is the world (Matt. 13:38)
   a. Your Macedonia begins at your door
   b. We all meet lost people everywhere we go
2. Have you even noticed that they are there?
3. See how Paul and Silas seized every opportunity in Macedonia
   a. How many opportunities have you seized today?
   b. How many people have you told of Jesus and His love?

III. **Conclusion**
A. *Do You Hear the Cries of Lost Ones Around You?*
B. *They Are Crying Out for Your Message Every Day*

Come, Lord Jesus

Bible Invitation Series Ends   *Revelation 22:20*

I. Introduction
   A. *Last Things in the Bible Are Important*
      1. The last promise is "I come quickly"
      2. The last invitation is "Amen. Even so, come, Lord Jesus"
   B. *The Last Invitation Is a Prayer*
      1. It is a prayer by John for Jesus to return
      2. H. A. Ironside: "Surely every believing heart can join in the apostle's prayer"
   C. *Why Did John Invite Jesus to Return?*

II. Body
   A. *John Had Seen the Results of the World's Rebellion*
      1. John had seen man at his worst
         a. He had been there when Jesus was rejected and betrayed
         b. He had stood at the cross when Christ was crucified
         c. He had known many of the martyrs and had been exiled for his faith
      2. Jesus had given John a panorama of prophecy, a view of the future
         a. He had witnessed a preview of the wrath of the Lamb (Rev. 6)
         b. He had been given a glimpse of the coming Great Tribulation
      3. John had inside information on things others only speculate about
         a. He had seen the rise of the beast and the false prophet (Rev. 13)
         b. He had seen previews of the Battle of Armageddon (Rev. 14)
      4. Having seen all of this violence, he longed for the return of the Prince of Peace
   B. *John Had Seen the Glory of Christ's Return*
      1. He had heard the "Come up hither" of Revelation 4:1 (a picture of the Rapture)

      a. He had seen visions of believers in heaven filled with praise

      b. He had heard the songs of the saints from every tribe and nation

   2. John had witnessed the marriage of the Lamb and His bride, the Church (Rev. 19)

      a. He had seen the Bridegroom on horseback returning to reign

      b. He had marveled at the majesty of KING OF KINGS AND LORD OF LORDS

   3. John had seen the new Jerusalem coming down out of heaven (Rev. 21)

   4. John had firsthand information about the rewards of Christ for His people (Rev. 22:12)

   5. John was ready for the vision to become reality . . . to take place

   6. John longed for that coming great day

  C. *John Wanted to See His Returning King*

   1. John had been exiled on that island long enough

   2. John had good reasons for longing daily for Christ's return

      a. He wanted to see Jesus

      b. He wanted to reminisce about their days on earth together

      c. He wanted to talk about the cross and the resurrection

   3. John wanted the new body that will never grow old that he will receive in the resurrection

   4. John wanted to hold those nail-scarred hands and meet his Savior face to face

III. Conclusion

  A. *Can You Pray John's Prayer with Confidence?*

  B. *Are You Ready for Jesus to Come?*

  C. *Invite Him into Your Life, Then You Can Invite Him to Return*

The Church of the Open Door

Revelation 3:7–13

I. **Introduction**
   A. *Letters from Jesus to Seven Churches*
      1. The letters contain both censure and commendation
      2. Smyrna and Philadelphia receive only praise
      3. The church at Philadelphia had great opportunities for service
   B. *The Church of Philadelphia in Practice and Prophecy*
      1. This describes any local church true to the Scriptures and the Savior
      2. It is usually thought to picture the faithful just before Christ's return
   C. *The Manner and Message of Christ Toward This Church*

II. **Body**
   A. *The Presentation of Christ to This Church (v. 7)*
      1. "He that is holy"
      2. We're to serve our holy God in an unholy world
      3. The last days are to be marked by a lack of holy living
         a. Like the days of Noah and Lot (Luke 17:26–30)
         b. Characterized by false teachers (2 Peter 2)
         c. A time of moral decline (2 Tim. 3)
      4. "He that is true"—Our Lord is unchanged when standards fall
      5. "He that hath the key of David"
         a. He will come to reign on David's throne (Luke 1:32)
         b. He will bring peace to this troubled world
   B. *The Promise of Christ to This Church (v. 8)*
      1. "I have set before thee an open door"
      2. A faithful church has great opportunities for service
         a. When Christ opens a door none can close it
         b. We will give an account of our service (Rom. 14:12; 1 Cor. 3:11–15)

41

       c. What doors has God opened for us? (Children? Youth? Missions?)

       d. Have we been faithful in going through them?

    3. With even a little strength we can be effective for Him

       a. God's power compensates for our weakness

       b. If we are faithful, He will keep opening doors

       c. Let us be ready to walk courageously through them

C. *The Prospects for the Future of This Church (vv. 9–11)*

    1. Even their enemies to respect them ultimately (v. 9)

    2. To be kept from the hour of trouble (Tribulation) (v. 10)

    3. To be encouraged by the blessed hope of Christ's return (v. 11)

    4. Crowns for their faithfulness at the Judgment Seat of Christ (v. 11)

    5. Rewards for overcomers (v. 12)

       a. Pillar in the temple; permanent recognition of victories

       b. Sharing in the blessing of the New Jerusalem

III. Conclusion

A. *This Message Is for Individuals, Not Just the Church*

B. *There Are Open Doors of Service for You and Me*

C. *There Are Rewards for Faithful You and Me*

A Cure for Heart Trouble

John 14:1–6

I. **Introduction**
 A. *Many People Have Troubled Hearts Today*
  1. Troubled over world events (Luke 21:23–28)
  2. Troubled over the breakup of so many homes
  3. Troubled about moral decline (Matt. 24:12)
  4. Troubled about violence (Matt. 24:37–38)
 B. *What Can We Do with Troubled Hearts?*
 C. *We Can Take Them to Jesus, Who Cures Them*

II. **Body**
 A. *Jesus Is the Cure for Unsettled Hearts (v. 1)*
  1. "Let not your heart be troubled"
  2. Why were the disciples troubled?
   a. One of them would soon betray Jesus (13:21)
   b. They would soon be separated from Jesus (13:36)
   c. Peter would soon deny Jesus (13:37–38)
  3. How could Jesus cure their unsettled hearts?
   a. One among them would fail, but Christ is always faithful
   b. One among them would be a liar, but Christ is always true
   c. They would soon witness death, but Christ is always the life
  4. Keeping their hearts focused on Christ would bring them peace
  5. This is as true today as in the Upper Room (Isa. 26:3)
 B. *Jesus Is the Cure for Uncertain Hearts (v. 4)*
  1. "We know not whither thou goest"
  2. The uncertainty of eternity
   a. Life's great question: "What lies beyond the grave?"
   b. The question of people through the ages
  3. Christ came to answer that question forever (v. 2)
   a. "In my Father's house are many mansions"
   b. "I go to prepare a place for you"

        c. "I will come again and receive you unto myself"

    4. There is no longer any need to be uncertain about eternity

C. *Jesus Is the Cure for the Unsaved Heart (v. 4–6)*

    1. "How can we know the way?"

    2. Thomas didn't want to miss out on heaven

        a. He wanted to be with Jesus forever

        b. He wanted to get in on those mansions

    3. Thomas expected a path and got a person—Jesus

    4. "I am the way, the truth, and the life" (the only way)

III. **Conclusion**

A. *Jesus Meets the Heart Needs of Every Sinner*

    1. The way: reconciliation for the estranged

    2. The truth: illumination for the mind darkened by sin

    3. The life: regeneration for the one dead in sin

B. *Let Jesus Come into Your Heart (Rev. 3:20)*

The God of Beginnings

Genesis 1:1–13

I. Introduction
- A. *God Is Eternal (v. 1)*
  1. In the beginning, God was already there (Deut. 33:27)
  2. God has always existed and will always exist (Isa. 43:10)
- B. *God Is at Work in a Chaotic World (v. 2)*
  1. The earth was without form and void
  2. Darkness was upon the face of the deep
  3. The Spirit of God moved to bring about change
  4. This is His purpose in our lives

II. Body
- A. *God Brings Light (vv. 3–5)*
  1. "Let there be light: and there was light" (v. 3)
  2. God is the source of light
     a. Exod. 34:28–35: Moses's face shone after being in God's presence
     b. Ps. 104:2: "Who coverest thyself with light as with a garment"
     c. Luke 2:9: "and the glory of the Lord shone round about them"
     d. Rev. 22:5: "and the Lamb is the light thereof"
  3. The sun and moon are but deputies to bring God's light to earth
  4. God wants to bring light to our lives through the gospel
  5. "I am the light of the world" (John 8:12)
  6. Let Christ take the darkness out of your life
- B. *God Brings Order (vv. 6–8)*
  1. The light of God has revealed the chaotic condition of the world
  2. Now there must be a dividing of the waters, the forming of the atmosphere
     a. Earth is being prepared for life
     b. The Holy Spirit brings order out of confusion
  3. When God wants order, He does some dividing

        a. The cross is a divider
        b. There is no neutral ground at the cross
    4. All humanity is divided like the two dying thieves at the cross (Luke 23:39–43)
        a. One thief realized his sin and accepted Christ as Savior and Lord
        b. The other thief rejected Christ and joined the crowd in mocking Him
        c. On which side of the cross are you?

C. *God Brings Life (vv. 9–13)*
    1. God divides the water and the land
        a. The seas, lakes, and rivers appear
        b. Planet Earth is soon to be a life-sustaining place
    2. The Creator calls for fruitfulness
        a. Plants and trees spring up at His command
        b. God also wants us to be fruitful (John 15:8)
    3. The fruit of the Spirit should be evident in each of us (Gal. 5:22–23)

III. Conclusion

A. *You Can Have a New Beginning, a New Birth (John 3:1–5)*

B. *Faith in Christ Will Make You a New Creation (2 Cor. 5:17)*

God's Plan for Both Creations

Genesis 1:3–31

I. Introduction
  A. *The Order and Divisions of the Six Days of Creation*
    1. Day one—light; day four—the sun and the moon
    2. Day two—waters divided; day five—water creatures
    3. Day three—land; day six—land animals and man
  B. *The Order of Creation Reveals the Creator's Purposes*

II. Body
  A. *What God Has He Desires to Share (vv. 3–5;14–19)*
    1. God, the source of light, deputizes the sun and the moon
      a. He could have created us to live in darkness
      b. He had light available and desired to share it
    2. God has many things He desires to share with us
      a. The light of life (Matt. 5:16)
      b. Peace (John 14:22)
      c. Eternal life (John 3:16; 5:24)
      d. His divine nature (2 Peter 1:4)
      e. His glory (John 17:21–23; Rom. 8:17–18)
      f. Heaven (John 14:1–3)
      g. His wisdom (James 1:14)
    3. All of these things are available to His new creatures (2 Cor. 5:17) through faith in His Son
    4. What are you doing without that God wants to share with you?
  B. *What God Begins He Determines to Continue (vv. 6–8; 20–23)*
    1. God created the earth to sustain life
      a. He could have left it only a place of beauty
      b. He could have left it a place of flowing water, rocks, and mountains
      c. He could have left it a place for angels to visit on vacation
    2. Creation was only the beginning: living creatures were also in the plan
    3. The new birth is only the beginning

      a. God continues His work in each believer (Phil. 1:6)

      b. He continues His work through circumstances (Rom. 8:28–29)

      c. He continues His work through His Word (Eph. 5:26–27)

      d. He continues His work through chastening (Heb. 12:5–7)

      e. He continues His work through the Holy Spirit (John 14:16–26)

  C. *What God Creates He Divinely Commissions (vv. 9–13; 24–28)*

    1. Creation obeys its Creator, each creature and plant reproducing after its kind

      a. This is evident at every birth

      b. Every newborn animal or person proclaims this truth

    2. Believers are also to reproduce

      a. This is called the Great Commission (Matt. 28:18–20)

      b. We are to be His witnesses (Acts 1:8)

    3. We have been commissioned to bring the lost to Him

III. **Conclusion**

  A. *Are You Allowing God's Purposes to Be Fulfilled in You?*

  B. *Isn't It Time You Surrendered to God's Wonderful Plan?*

What's Wrong with Everybody?

Genesis 1:26–27; 3

I. **Introduction**
   A. *What Is Man?*
      1. This is one of life's most basic questions
      2. Is man the product of millions of years of evolution?
      3. Is man a special creation of God?
   B. *What Is Wrong with Everybody?*
      1. The philosopher's question
      2. The psychologist's question
      3. The criminologist's question
   C. *The Bible Answers These Important Questions*

II. **Body**
   A. *Man Was Created in the Image of God (1:26–27)*
      1. "So God created man in his own image"
         a. Created from the dust of the ground (2:7)
         b. The crowning work of God's creation
         c. To have dominion over the earth (1:26)
      2. What is meant by "the image of God?"
         a. Like God, Adam had intellect, emotion, and will
         b. These are the requirements of personhood
         c. Adam and Eve were also without sin
      3. God placed Adam and Eve in a perfect environment (Eden)
   B. *Adam Fell Through Sin, Marring the Image (3:1–6)*
      1. There was one forbidden fruit in the Garden of Eden
         a. How gracious and giving God had been!
         b. Adam and Eve chose to disobey their Lord
         c. In their taking of the forbidden fruit, the whole human race fell into sin
      2. We are all sinners and act like it (Rom. 3:10–23)
         a. Experience teaches us that we are sinners
         b. Newspaper headlines announce that we are sinners

        c. Crime's deadly march screams that we are sinners

    3. Human efforts to remedy the situation fail

        a. Education and legislation fail

        b. Prosecution and punishment fail

C. *Through Grace, the Second Adam Restores the Image*

    1. Adam's disobedience plunged us all into sin (Rom. 5:12)

    2. Christ's obedience makes salvation available to all (Rom. 5:18–19)

        a. His death redeems us (Eph. 1:7)

        b. His resurrection guarantees that He lives to keep us (Rom. 1:4; Heb. 7:25)

        c. His Spirit dwells within to enable us to live righteously (1 Cor. 6:19–20)

III. **Conclusion**

A. *The Purpose of God in Creation Is Realized in Salvation*

    1. We have fellowship with God through faith in Christ (1 John 1:3)

    2. Living in fellowship with God brings real joy (1 John 1:4)

B. *Christ Is the Answer for What's Wrong with Everybody*

What Do We Need?

I. **Introduction**
   A. *People Are Confused About What They Need*
      1. Lifetimes are spent gathering temporary trinkets
      2. What profit is there in gaining the whole world (Mark 8:36)?
      3. We all leave this world empty-handed (1 Tim. 6:7)
   B. *God Knows Our Basic Needs and Provides for Them*
      1. See how God provided for our needs in His creative plan
      2. We must go back to the beginning to discover our basic needs today

II. **Body**
   A. *We Need Food (vv. 8–14)*
      1. Paul said food and clothing ought to make us content (1 Tim. 6:8)
      2. God placed His newly created man in a beautiful garden
         a. It contained all manner of trees and plants for his delightful diet
         b. Beauty and bounty were his for the taking
      3. In spite of this ideal environment, Adam fell into sin
         a. This shows that our need is not a new berth but a new birth
         b. Adam disobeyed in spite of God's love and provision
      4. We also need spiritual food
         a. "Man shall not live by bread alone" (Matt. 4:4)
         b. "Desire the sincere milk of the word" (1 Peter 2:2)
      5. God has graciously provided food for the body and the soul
   B. *We Need to Be Faithful (vv. 15–17)*
      1. God gave Adam the responsibility of taking care of the garden

         a. We all need responsibilities in life; we need to work

         b. In the path of duty, we stumble onto happiness

      2. Thank God for work and the strength to do it

      3. We also need to be faithful to God, obeying His will

         a. Every tree but one was for food

         b. The one exception became Adam's downfall

      4. What is your area of temptation and battle?

      5. Focus on all that you have in Christ, and victory will be yours

  C. *We Need Fellowship (vv. 18–25)*

      1. "It is not good that man should be alone"

      2. The one thing about creation that was not good was man's lack of a mate

      3. God created woman to remedy this problem

         a. God performed the first surgery and used the first anesthesia

         b. God made woman from Adam's rib; how fitting!

      4. Now Adam wouldn't have to be alone anymore

      5. Marriage is the closest bond of life, the most blessed fellowship

      6. We also need the fellowship of other believers (Heb. 10:25)

III. **Conclusion**

  A. *God Has Provided for Our Physical, Spiritual, and Social Needs*

  B. *He Has Also Provided Forgiveness of Sins and Eternal Life*

  C. *God Wants to Meet You in Your Special Need Today*

The Colt, the Crowd, and the Children

Series on the Cross Begins   *Matthew 21:1–16*

I. **Introduction**
   A. *Jesus and His Disciples Approaching Jerusalem*
      1. This marked the beginning of the end . . . and the new beginning
         a. The trial and crucifixion of Christ lay ahead
         b. Then would come the resurrection and the birth of the Church
      2. Thousands of people were gathered in Jerusalem for Passover
   B. *The Triumphal Entry into Jerusalem About to Take Place*
   C. *The Disciples, the Donkey, and the Details*
      1. The colt to be brought by the disciples
      2. The crowd's praises and palm branches
      3. The children, who were wiser than them all

II. **Body**
   A. *The Colt (vv. 2–7)*
      1. Jesus gave His disciples a strange instruction
         a. Go to the village and find a colt tied
         b. They were to loose the unbroken colt and bring it to Jesus
         c. Their answer to any who questioned them was to be "The Lord needs him"
      2. We are to bring to Jesus those with unbroken wills
      3. The stubborn will of the unbroken colt submitted to Jesus
         a. The submission of the colt is a picture of the coming kingdom of Christ
         b. When He comes to set up His kingdom, Christ will ride again (Rev. 19:11–16)
   B. *The Crowd (vv. 8–11)*
      1. The multitude spread their garments before Jesus
      2. They placed palm branches along the way (Palm Sunday)
      3. The crowd praised the Lord
         a. "Hosanna to the son of David"

        b. "Blessed is he that cometh in the name of the Lord"

        c. "Hosanna in the highest"

    4. How fickle crowds can be with their praise!

        a. Soon the cheers became jeers

        b. Soon the blessings became boos

        c. Soon the "Crown Him" became "Crucify Him"

C. *The Children (vv. 12–16)*

    1. The cleansing of the temple

    2. Jesus healing the blind and the lame

    3. The anger of the Lord's enemies

    4. The praise of the children (v. 16)

    5. The importance of reaching children for the Lord

    6. The Lord's pleasure at praising children

III. Conclusion

A. *Is Your Will Surrendered to the Savior?*

B. *Are You Occupied with His Praise?*

C. *Do You Have Childlike Faith?*

D. *Are You as Wise as These Children?*

Peter's Path to Power

Series on the Cross   *Luke 22:31–32, 60–61*

I. **Introduction**
   A. *Peter's Denials of Christ*
      1. We understand ourselves better when we understand Peter
      2. We can identify with his failures and successes
   B. *Coming Tough Times for the Disciples*
      1. Jesus had told them of His coming suffering (v. 15)
      2. He had just revealed His betrayal by one of them (v. 21)
      3. He had told Peter that he would be attacked by Satan (v. 31)
   C. *What Changed This Denying Disciple into a Dynamic Christian?*

II. **Body**
   A. *The Prayer of Christ for Peter (v. 31)*
      1. The Lord was concerned for Peter when he was tempted
         a. "Satan hath desired to have thee" (v. 30)
         b. "I have prayed for thee that thy faith fail not"
      2. Satan desires to defeat all believers
      3. Jesus is still praying for His tempted ones
         a. Jesus prayed for us in Gethsemane (John 17:20)
         b. He intercedes for us now in heaven (Heb. 7:25)
      4. Peter lost his battle with temptation, but his faith didn't fail
         a. Jesus commissioned him to strengthen the others after this crisis
         b. He became the key spokesman for his Lord on Pentecost (Acts 2)
   B. *The Precise Time of the Cock's Crowing When Peter Failed (v. 60)*
      1. The time of this rooster's crowing had been prophesied (v. 34)
      2. We have a few good words for a rooster

        a. He rises early and goes about his God-given task
        b. He does that work without praise
        c. He awakens sleepers
        d. He is a proclaimer of good news
        e. He never gets bored with the same routine
    3. God used this particular rooster to bring Peter to repentance
        a. His timely crowing reminded Peter of his promise to Jesus
        b. His crowing also reminded Peter of the Lord's promise to him
  C. *The Lord's Powerful Look at Peter (v. 61)*
    1. The Lord turned and looked at Peter
    2. With all that was happening to Jesus, He still cared for Peter
    3. We can only speculate about that look
        a. Was it a look of rebuke, pity, or grief?
        b. What was the heart of Jesus communicating to Peter?
    4. That look broke Peter's heart and sent him out weeping

III.   Conclusion
  A. *Peter Was Down That Denying Day, but He Was Not Out*
  B. *The Love of Christ Would Draw Him Back and Give Him Hope*
    1. God met Peter where he was and made him what he ought to be
    2. He wants to do the same for you, even if you have failed Him

The Cross, the Cure

Series on the Cross   *1 Corinthians 1:18*

I. **Introduction**
   A. *What Does the Cross Have to Do with a Troubled Church?*
      1. The church at Corinth was a troubled church
         a. Immorality was common among the members
         b. Carnal divisions were destroying the church
      2. Paul chose the preaching of the cross as the remedy for this condition
      3. Facing the cost of the cross can bring personal revival
   B. *The Preaching of the Cross Meets Us Where We Live*

II. **Body**
   A. *The Cross Is the Cure for Divisions (vv. 10–18)*
      1. The Corinthian Christians had become followers of men ·
         a. Some said they followed Paul, some Apollos, and some Cephas
         b. Some said they rejected men and followed Christ
      2. Paul removed himself from the center of attention (v. 13)
         a. Was Paul crucified for you?
         b. Were you baptized in the name of Paul?
      3. The focus of faith must be on the One on the cross
         a. Consider the sufferings of Calvary (Luke 23:33–46)
         b. Remember the thorns, the nails, and the spear
      4. How petty our divisions become in light of the sufferings of Christ
      5. Calvary ought to end all divisions and unite a church in serving Jesus
   B. *The Cross Is the Cure for the Dying (v. 18)*
      1. The message of the cross seems foolish to those who are perishing
         a. Perishing because they are sinners (Rom. 3:10–23)

   b.   Perishing because they will not come to Christ
        (John 5:40)
   c.   Perishing because they will not believe (John
        3:36)
2.   Many religious people are perishing
   a.   Good works cannot keep one from perishing
        (Isa. 64:6)
   b.   Keeping the law cannot keep one from
        perishing (Gal. 2:21)
   c.   Religious ceremonies cannot keep one from
        perishing (John 1:13)
3.   Only receiving the message of the cross by faith
     saves from perishing
   a.   "Unto us which are saved it is the power of
        God"
   b.   Christ died on the cross that we might have
        eternal life (Isa. 53:5–6)
4.   Are you certain of salvation?
C.   *The Cross Is the Cure for the Doubting (vv. 19–25)*
   1.   Paul calls in the doubters: the worldly-wise, the
        questioners, and the religious leaders
   2.   Their arguments fail in light of the death of Christ
        and His resurrection
   3.   Honest investigation of the cross and the
        resurrection removes all doubts
      a.   Christ died for our sins, making justification
           possible (Rom. 3:23–28)
      b.   His resurrection is the guarantee of our
           salvation (Rom. 1:4)

III. Conclusion
   A.   *Churches That Focus on the Cross Experience Unity
        and Revival*
   B.   *Believers Who Focus on the Cross Find It Easy to
        Forgive*
   C.   *Sinners Who Come to the Christ of the Cross Find
        Salvation*

Meet Christ and His Crucifiers

Series on the Cross Ends   *Acts 2:22–24*

I. **Introduction**
   A. *The Arrival of the Day of Pentecost*
      1. The day the promise of the Father was fulfilled (Acts 1:4)
      2. The day the Holy Spirit came to dwell within all believers (Acts 1:5–8)
   B. *Looking Back to the Cross from this Vantage Point*
      1. Peter's sermon that day was of Christ crucified
      2. Peter introduced his hearers to Christ and His crucifiers
      3. We have this responsibility every time we preach
   C. *The Players in History's Greatest Drama*

II. **Body**
   A. *Meet the Man (v. 22)*
      1. Peter wanted everyone to know Christ
         a. He wanted them to know the perfect Man
         b. Even Pilate had been unable to find any fault in Him (John 18:38–19:6)
      2. Peter wanted everyone to know the Man approved of His Father
         a. He had always been about His Father's business (Luke 2:49)
         b. The Father had voiced His approval from heaven at His baptism (Matt. 3:16–17)
      3. Peter wanted everyone to know the miracle Man
         a. The Man who was "approved of God among you by wonders and signs"
         b. The Man who had healed the sick and raised the dead
         c. The Man who had demonstrated His power over nature (Matt. 8:23–27)
   B. *Meet the Man with the Plan (vv. 23–24)*
      1. The cross was no afterthought with God
         a. He was "delivered by the determinate counsel and foreknowledge of God"

        b. Christ was not a victim on the cross but a
           victor
   2. Peter built his sermon on the prophetic Scriptures
      (vv. 16–23)
      a. He called on the prophet Joel to prove his
        point
      b. He declared that the outpouring of the Spirit at
        Pentecost had been prophesied
      c. He told them of signs in nature yet to come
   3. Peter announced that the resurrection had taken
      place
      a. He declared Jesus, "Whom God hath raised
        up"
      b. The power of death was overcome
      c. The grave could not hold Him
   4. What good news this is for us all!
 C. *Meet the Mean Crucifiers of the Man (vv. 23–24)*
   1. Christ was taken prisoner like a common criminal
      a. Christ was betrayed and arrested (Luke
        22:47–53)
      b. The judge of all the earth was made to stand
        before an earthly judge (John 19:28–40)
   2. Christ was beaten and crucified while His accusers
      cursed and spat upon Him
   3. Christ fulfilled the prophecies of His death for
      sinners (Isa. 53:5–6)
   4. Even on the cross, He was the Man of forgiveness
      (Luke 23:34)

III. Conclusion
 A. *The Son of Man Came to Seek and to Save the Lost*
   (Luke 19:10)
 B. *Christ Offers Salvation Through Faith Alone to You*
   and Me

The Broken Seal

Matthew 27:62–66; 28:11–15

I. Introduction

A. *The Resurrection of Christ Had Been Promised to His Disciples*
  1. Both His death and His resurrection are clearly explained (Matt. 20:18–19)
  2. Neither His death nor His resurrection should have taken them by surprise

B. *The Enemies of Christ Remembered, but His Disciples Forgot*
  1. At the cross, His disciples forsook Christ and fled
  2. Matthew Henry on this strange development: "Hate is keener sighted than love."

C. *The Priests and Pharisees Pleaded to Pilate for a Watch*

II. Body

A. *The Enemies of Christ Were Correct About His Promise (vv. 60–63)*
  1. Let's think about the body of Jesus
     a. From Mary's touch in the manger to the misery of the cross
     b. The abuse He took in His body for you and me (Isa. 53; Matt. 27:26–54)
  2. Nicodemas and wealthy Joseph laid the body of Jesus in the tomb
  3. The enemies of Jesus still feared that bleeding, breathless body
     a. They remembered His promise: "After three days I will rise again" (v. 63)
     b. This promise was made repeatedly: John 2:22–23; Matt. 12:39–40; 17:9
  4. They knew that He had promised a bodily resurrection, not just a spiritual resurrection
     a. Who would ask for a guard and a sealed tomb to prevent a spiritual resurrection?
     b. Who would try to seal a spirit in a cave?

     5. Strangely, they called Jesus a deceiver, yet they feared that He might really rise again

  B. *The Enemies of Christ Were Concerned About His Promise (v. 64)*

     1. They wanted the sepulchre sealed and guarded until the third day

     2. They also feared that His disciples might hatch a plot to make it appear that He had risen

     3. They trembled at the impact on the public if word got out that He was alive

       a. Everyone has thought of death and wanted it overcome by life

       b. Word of a resurrection would be the most powerful news ever received

     4. This is exactly what happened when Christ arose

       a. The resurrection became the message of all New Testament preaching

       b. As a result, the world was turned upside down for Christ (Acts 17:6)

  C. *The Enemies of Christ Were Conquered by His Promise (vv. 65–66)*

     1. Pilate granted the guard and had his soldiers seal the tomb

       a. A heavy rope was placed across the stone

       b. The seal of the Roman Empire was placed on it

     2. Pilate's soldiers and seal could not keep Christ from His promised resurrection

     3. The broken seal became a great proof of the promised resurrection (28:11–15)

       a. Roman soldiers did not sleep at their posts

       b. Sleeping on watch would have cost them their lives

       c. The story to discredit the resurrection was itself discredited

     4. Christ arose! The promise was fulfilled! (28:1–10)

III. Conclusion

  A. *The Broken Seal Guarantees the Resurrection*

  B. *The Resurrection Guarantees the Deity of Christ*

  C. *His Promises Guarantee the Salvation of All Who Trust Him*

Preparing Peter for Pentecost

John 21

I. **Introduction**
   A. *Peter Went from the Greatest Failure to the Greatest Firebrand*
      1. Denied his Lord three times by a fire
      2. Declared his Lord on Pentecost in the fire and power of the Holy Spirit
   B. *Peter Decided to Go Fishing*
      1. He has often been criticized for this post-resurrection fishing trip
      2. The others decided to go with him. (Our decisions affect others.)
   C. *Three Questions from Christ Prepared Peter for Pentecost*

II. **Body**
   A. *The Simple Question That Asked for the Facts (v. 5)*
      1. "Children, have ye any meat?"
      2. They were a group of hungry, tired, and discouraged disciples
         a. They had fished all night and caught nothing
         b. Many of us are like them—defeated and exhausted
      3. Jesus called to the disciples, asking His life-changing question
         a. "Have you any meat?" (Have you caught any fish?)
         b. He might have asked a less pointed question: "How is the boat holding up?"
      4. Jesus already knew the answer, but He wanted them to tell Him their needs
         a. He knows how things are in our lives, but He longs to have us tell Him
         b. Before we can be saved, we must admit that we are lost
         c. Before He can fill us, we must admit that we are empty

   B. *The Searching Question That Asked for First Place*
      (v. 15)
1. "Lovest thou me more than these?"
2. He asked this of Peter, the one who thought that he had lost his usefulness
3. He called Peter by his old name; He met Peter where he considered himself to be
4. He asked Peter if he loved Him more than the things around him
    a. Do you love me more than the sea?
    b. Do you love me more than your boat?
    c. Do you love me more than these nets, which used to mean so much to you?
    d. Do you love me more than these fish?
    e. Do you love me more than these friends?
5. This question, asked three times, corresponded to Peter's three denials of Christ

   C. *The Stern Question That Asked Peter to Follow Him*
      (vv. 21–22)
1. Christ told Peter that he was to feed the Lord's sheep and then die as a martyr
2. "Follow me": Peter had heard that call before and responded to it
3. Peter was concerned about what John was to do for Christ
    a. The Lord's answer: "What is that to thee?"
    b. Then He gave that familiar call again: "Follow thou me"
4. Following Christ is an individual matter, not dependent on what others do

III. Conclusion
   A. *Jesus Will Meet Us Where We Are*
   B. *Jesus Insists on Having First Place in Our Lives*
   C. *Jesus Calls Us to Follow Him, Regardless of What Others Do*
   D. *How Will You Answer Our Lord's Three Questions of Commitment?*

The Power of a Loving Church

Acts 2:41–46

I. **Introduction**
  A. *Meet the Powerful First Church of Jerusalem*
    1. The promise of Pentecost was fulfilled (Acts 1:5–8)
    2. Thousands were converted on that special occasion (Acts 2)
  B. *What Gave That Dynamic Church Its Power?*
    1. The members modeled God's love to the world
    2. This love changed their lives and empowered their witness

II. **Body**
  A. *They Loved the Lord (vv. 41–42)*
    1. "They that gladly received his word were baptized"
      a. They responded to God's message of love (the gospel)
      b. They evidenced their love for God through baptism
    2. Communion and baptism show God's love
      a. Communion speaks of Christ's death (1 Cor. 11:23–26)
      b. Baptism speaks of His burial and resurrection (Rom. 6:3–4)
    3. Baptism shows our love for Christ
      a. Baptism is following Jesus (Matt. 3:15–17)
      b. Baptism is obeying Jesus (Matt. 28:18–20)
      c. Baptism is identifying with Jesus (Acts 2:41)
  B. *They Loved One Another (vv. 42–46)*
    1. "In the apostle's doctrine"
      a. They loved to gather to hear God's Word
      b. Today the tendency is to gather less (Heb. 10:25)
    2. "In fellowship"
      a. This is a great reason for gathering to worship
      b. Christians should love one another
      c. The closest bond is that we are members of His body (1 Cor. 12)

    3. "In breaking of bread"

        a. Sharing communion and remembering Christ's death

        b. Speaking of Christ's love at the cross

    4. "In prayers"

        a. Building love for one another

        b. Sharing needs and rejoicing in God's provision

C. *They Loved Lost People (v. 47)*

    1. They were constantly witnessing and praising God

    2. The Lord added to the church daily

    3. We are all to be involved in outreach

    4. The whole church is to be a team to reach the world

III. Conclusion

    A. *What Did the Jerusalem Church Have That We Lack?*

    B. *Is the Power of Love Active Among Us?*

    C. *What Can We Do to Increase Our Love?*

        a. Our love for the Lord

        b. Our love for one another

Hell: What's It All About?

I. **Introduction**
  A. *The Gentle Jesus Rebuked Sinners*
    1. Some people speak only of God's love
    2. Some people think that God's love excuses sinners
    3. But Jesus warned sinners of the wrath to come (Matt. 3:7)
  B. *This Raises Questions About Hell and Judgment*
    1. Can hell be real?
    2. Can a loving God allow sinners to go to hell?
    3. Can hell last forever?

II. **Body**
  A. *The Bible Speaks to Those Who Are Destined for Hell (vv. 20–21)*
    1. "Woe unto thee"
    2. On whom were these woes pronounced?
      a. On those who did not repent of their sins
      b. On those who had rejected Christ and His words
      c. On those to whom much light had been given
    3. We are all deserving of hell
      a. We are all sinners (Rom. 3:10–23; Isa. 64:6)
      b. Christ died to save sinners from hell (Rom. 5:8; 10:9)
    4. Rejecting Christ brings the wrath of God (John 3:36)
    5. Jesus described the suffering of hell (Luke 16:19–31)
  B. *The Bible Reveals Degrees of Punishment in Hell (vv. 21–24)*
    1. "More tolerable for Tyre and Sidon" (v. 22)
    2. "More tolerable for Sodom" (v. 24; Matt. 10:15)
    3. Dr. John R. Rice: "Notice the doctrine in verses 22 and 24 that there will be degrees of punishment in the judgment and therefore in hell" (*The King of the Jews* [Murfreesboro, Tenn.: Sword of the Lord, 1955]).

    4.　Degrees of punishment are based on one's opportunity

      a.　Chorazin and Bethsaida received and rejected much light

      b.　Tyre, Sidon, and Sodom were given less light

    5.　These words of Jesus rule out annihilation of the lost

  C.　*The Bible Declares the Duration of Hell (25:41)*

    1.　It is "everlasting fire prepared for the devil and his angels"

    2.　There is a difference in degree but not in duration

    3.　Hell is no Protestant purgatory

    4.　What about hell and the future of the satanic trinity (Rev. 20:10–15)?

      a.　The Devil, the beast, and the false prophet are judged

      b.　They are cast into the lake of fire forever

      c.　Those who are not in the book of life will join them

    5.　Why spend eternity with your worst enemy?

III.　Conclusion

  A.　*How to Avoid Hell*

    1.　Come with your sins to Jesus

    2.　Receive Him by faith as your Lord and Savior

  B.　*Spend Eternity with the One Who Died to Save You from Hell*

Satan:
His Personality, His Perversion, and His Purpose

Ezekiel 28:12–15; Isaiah 14:12–17

I. **Introduction**
   A. *How the World Sees Satan*
      1. Horns, a red suit, a tail
      2. A kick for cartoons—shoveling coal in hell
   B. *How False Impressions Play into Our Enemy's Hands*
   C. *How We Can Unmask Our Ancient Foe*

II. **Body**
   A. *Satan's Personality (v. 12)*
      1. Ezekiel lamented the king of Tyrus
         a. His description goes beyond the king
         b. Bible scholars believe this to be an accepted portrayal of Satan
      2. Satan is full of wisdom and perfect in beauty
         a. Surprising qualities in one now so evil
         b. Shows the destructive nature of sin
      3. Satan's abilities prove him to be a person
         a. Able to speak (Gen. 3)
         b. Able to appear before God (Job 1)
         c. Able to quote Scripture (Matt. 4)
      4. Satan now uses his abilities to destroy (John 10:10; 1 Peter 5:6)
   B. *Satan's Perversion of Good Things (vv. 13–15)*
      1. His perversion of wisdom in Eden (Gen. 3)
         a. This was a tree to make one wise (Gen. 3)
         b. "Your eyes shall be opened"
         c. "Ye shall be as gods"
         d. This perversion has continued (Rom. 1:22)
      2. His perversion of beauty (v. 13)
         a. The precious stones remind us of heaven (Rev. 21:18–21)
         b. Now Satan deceives people to keep them from heaven
         c. He often uses man's lust for earthly treasures to keep him from heaven

69

    3. His perversion of music (v. 13)
       a. Music should glorify God
       b. Satan uses it to glorify sin and himself
  C. *Satan's Purposes (Isa. 14:12–15)*
    1. Here is another description of Satan and his fall
    2. He desires to weaken the nations (v. 12)
    3. He desires to take God's place (vv. 13–14)
       a. This is his goal in temptation
       b. It was his purpose in Eden and is still his purpose now
    4. Satan will go to any length to accomplish his evil purposes
       a. He will lie and deceive (John 8:44; Rev. 20:10)
       b. Don't let him deceive you

III. Conclusion
  A. *Christ Came to Give Life; Satan Seeks to Destroy*
  B. *Choose the One Whom You Will Serve*

The Wrath of God

Job 36:18; Romans 1:18; 2:5

I. **Introduction**
   A. *These Are Two Subjects to Which We Do Not Do Justice*
      1. God's love is beyond our knowledge
      2. God's wrath is beyond our comprehension
   B. *Is It Right to Preach About God's Wrath?*
      1. It is right to warn people to flee a burning building
      2. It is right to point out the warning signs of a deadly disease
      3. We are obligated to warn about these real dangers
   C. *What Can We Know About the Wrath of God?*

II. **Body**
   A. *The Wrath of God Is Real (Job 36:18)*
      1. The Bible declares that the wrath of God is real
      2. Psalms offers many references to God's wrath
         a. "Then shall he speak to them in his wrath" (Ps. 2:5)
         b. "The Lord shall swallow them up in his wrath" (Ps. 21:9)
         c. "The wrath of God came upon them" (Ps. 78:31)
      3. Jesus warned: "Flee from the wrath to come" (Matt. 3:7)
      4. God's wrath abides on those who reject Christ (John 3:36)
   B. *The Wrath of God Is Revealed (Rom. 1:18)*
      1. God has not hidden His wrath
         a. His wrath was revealed in the flood (Gen. 6–8)
         b. His wrath was revealed in the destruction of Sodom and Gomorrah (Gen. 19)
      2. God's wrath was revealed against the nations
         a. Against Israel in sin at Sinai (Exod. 32:10)
         b. Against wicked Gentile nations (Ezek. 25–26)
      3. God's wrath was revealed at the cross
         a. Jesus took our place to save us from that wrath (Rom. 5:9)

        b. "My God, My God, why hast thou forsaken
           me?" (Matt. 27:46)

    C. *The Wrath of God Is Reserved (Rom. 2:5)*
      1. The privilege of storing up heavenly treasure
         (Matt. 6:20)
         a. We can also store up wrath
         b. "Treasurest up unto thyself wrath" (Rom. 2:5)
      2. A day of wrath is coming (Rev. 6:17)
      3. God will show His wrath during the Tribulation
         period (Rev. 14:14–20)
      4. He will show His wrath in the seven last plagues
         (Rev. 15)
      5. He will show His wrath in the pouring out of the
         seven vials (Rev. 16)
      6. He will show His wrath in the judgment of the
         great white throne (Rev. 20:11–15)

III. **Conclusion**
    A. *Jonathan Edwards's "Sinners in the Hands of an*
       Angry God"
      1. Edwards's preaching wakened his church and
         launched a great awakening
      2. Do we need more preaching on God's wrath?
    B. *A Prophet Cried for Mercy in the Day of Wrath (Zeph.*
       2:1–3)
    C. *Flee Now to Christ, and Escape the Wrath to Come*
    D. *Jesus Will Receive You Just as You Are*

The Path to Perversion

Romans 1:20–32

I. Introduction
A. *A Sad Story of the Perversion of Public Practice*
   1. A people religiously perverted (vv. 24–25)
   2. A people morally perverted (vv. 26–27)
   3. A people intellectually perverted (vv. 28–32)
B. *What Caused This Tragedy?*
   1. Why would people fall so far from truth?
   2. What went wrong?

II. Body
A. *They Forgot God's Position (v. 21)*
   1. "They glorified him not as God"
   2. They did this even though they knew God
      a. They did not give Him first place in their lives
      b. They chose a dangerous way to live
   3. Is Christ Lord of your life?
      a. Is the Lord of the planets the Lord of your plans?
      b. Is the Lord of the tempests the Lord of your tongue?
      c. Is the Lord of the heavens the Lord of your home?
      d. Is the Lord of the ages the Lord of your agenda?
   4. Christ must have the preeminence in our lives (Col. 1:18)
   5. He deserves to be first in our hearts
B. *They Forgot God's Provision (v. 21)*
   1. "Neither were [they] thankful"
   2. Ingratitude affected their uplook and then their outlook
   3. They became "vain in their imaginations"
      a. They took credit for all that God had given them
      b. They became proud of their supposed accomplishments
   4. Pride darkened their hearts to the light of life

73

         a.   They became self-centered
         b.   They should have been Christ centered
    C.   *They Forgot God's Personality (vv. 22–32)*
       1.   "Professing themselves to be wise they became
           fools"
         a.   They questioned the Creator
         b.   They rejected the evidence of His creative plan
       2.   Rejecting the Creator led to idolatry
         a.   They made images of people and animals
         b.   They exalted the creation above the Creator
       3.   Idolatry takes the form of the age in which it exists
       4.   Idolatry led to immorality
         a.   Homosexuality became rampant
         b.   They became slaves to sin

III.   **Conclusion**
    A.   *Two Paths Stretch Before Us—to Paradise or to*
       Perversion
    B.   *Choose Christ, the Path to Paradise*

A Sermon for Tough Times

Psalm 121:1–2; John 4:35; Luke 21:28

I. **Introduction**
  A. *We've Come Through Some Tough Times*
    1. ˙ Sickness and death have entered some of our homes
    2. Tough economic conditions have discouraged us
    3. Church attendance has declined
  B. *What Can We Do?*

II. **Body**
  A. *We Can Lift Up Our Eyes for Help (Ps. 121)*
    1. The psalmist was in trouble
      a. He worried day and night
      b. He feared that he was slipping into danger
    2. He decided to look up
      a. He looked up to his omnipotent Creator (v. 2)
      b. He looked up to his omnipresent Lord (vv. 3–4)
      c. He looked up to his compassionate Savior (vv. 5–6)
      d. He looked up to his guarding God (vv. 7–8)
    3. We have looked to the Lord to save us (Isa. 45:22)
    4. We can look to our Lord to keep us (Heb. 13:5–6)
  B. *We Can Lift Up Our Eyes to the Harvest (John 4:35)*
    1. Let us lift up our eyes and see lost and perishing souls
      a. Our problems are small in contrast to their plight
      b. What could be worse than being bound for hell?
      c. No wonder Jesus calls on us to lift up our eyes!
    2. Let's look to the harvest, not to our hurts
      a. In doing so, we'll solve many of our problems
      b. A missionary vision eliminates self-pity
    3. Reaching people for Christ brings joy to troubled believers
      a. Those who sow in tears reap in joy (Ps. 126:5)
      b. Reaping turns us from sorrow to singing (Ps. 126:6)

   C. *We Can Lift Up Our Eyes for His Coming (Luke 21:28)*
     1. The last days will be characterized by trouble (Luke 21:25–26)
      a. Trouble in nature: earthquakes and storms
      b. Trouble in the nations: tensions and war
     2. Tough times are ahead for Planet Earth
      a. Christians have a message for tough times
      b. On the darkest day, God makes a way
     3. Tough times are temporary
      a. This is true prophetically: Christ will come
      b. This is true in daily life: all things pass (1 Peter 1:6–7)

III. Conclusion
   A. *Our Tough Times Have Not Taken God by Surprise*
   B. *Citizens of Heaven Should Not Be Looking Downward (Phil. 3:20–21)*
   C. *We Must Be About Our Father's Business*

It's About Time

1 Chronicles 12:32

I. Introduction
   A. *It Was a Time of Upheaval and Change for Israel*
     1. Saul had committed suicide in battle (10:4–6)
     2. David had been anointed king (11:1–3)
   B. *Who Knew What to Do at That Difficult Time?*
     1. The valuable children of Issachar knew what to do
     2. They had an understanding of the times
   C. *What Are We to Do in These Stressful Times?*

II. Body
   A. *We Are to Read the Signs of the Times (Matt. 16:1–4)*
     1. The Pharisees couldn't read the signs of the times
       a. Jesus said that they were but weather prophets
       b. They were looking for some miraculous sign
       c. They overlooked the obvious: Christ was there
     2. Beware of those who claim spectacular knowledge
       a. When Christ will return
       b. The identity of the Antichrist
     3. Look for signs already revealed in the Bible
       a. Moral decline as in the days of Noah (Luke 17:27)
       b. Violent eruptions in nature (Luke 21:25)
       c. International signs relating to Israel (Luke 21:29)
     4. Understanding these signs should help us win people to Christ
   B. *We Are to Recognize Special Times (Luke 19:44)*
     1. Jesus wept over the tough times coming to Jerusalem
       a. The city would be surrounded by enemies
       b. Desolation and destruction were ahead
     2. What were the reasons for His tears?
       a. Jerusalem had rejected Him in spite of having been given great light
       b. They had failed to recognize this special time (their day)
     3. Is this a special time in your life?

   a. Is God making you aware of your sins?
   b. Don't grieve Christ by not recognizing your opportunity to receive Him
  C. *We Are to Redeem These Sinful Times (Eph. 5:16)*
   1. "Redeeming the time, because the days are evil"
   2. Seizing opportunities to witness
    a. Making soul winning our priority
    b. Seeing people as God sees them
   3. Seeing iniquity abound in the last days (Matt. 24:12)
   4. Being lights in this dark world (Phil. 2:15)

III. **Conclusion**
  A. *It's Time to Wake Up (Rom. 13:11)*
  B. *We Know What to Do—So Let's Do It!*

Why Worship on Sunday?

I. Introduction
  A. *Most Christians Worship on Sunday*
  B. *Why Has Sunday Become the Day of Worship?*
  C. *What Are the Bible Reasons for Public Worship on Sunday?*

II. Body
  A. *Sunday Was the Day of the Resurrection (Luke 24:1)*
   1. The resurrection proved the deity of Christ (Rom. 1:4)
   2. There would be no church without the resurrection (1 Cor. 15:14)
   3. There would be no salvation without the resurrection (1 Cor. 15:17)
   4. The resurrection authenticated the teachings of Christ (John 2:18–21)
    a. His answer to those seeking a sign of authority
    b. Resurrection a fitting day to teach His Word
   5. Sunday is a great day to gather to celebrate new life
  B. *Sunday Was the Day of Worship for Early Christians (Acts 20:7)*
   1. What makes a day of worship?
    a. A day to pray and preach the gospel
    b. A day to fellowship with believers and celebrate Communion
    c. A day to give offerings to the Lord
   2. The first day of the week was for Communion and preaching (Acts 20:7)
   3. The first day of the week was for bringing offerings to the church (1 Cor. 16:2)
   4. Why did early Christians go to the temple on Saturday?
    a. On Saturday they evangelized at the temple
    b. On Sunday they worshiped in church meetings
    c. On Sunday we follow their example in public worship

C. *Sunday Commemorates Deliverance from the Law (Gal. 2:16)*
1. Christ died to deliver us from the law (Gal. 2:21)
2. No one can be justified by keeping the law (Gal. 3:11)
3. We are saved by grace through faith (Eph. 2:8–9)
    a. No amount of law keeping or other works can save us
    b. We ought to celebrate being free from the law
4. Grace calls for a higher standard than the law (Rom. 7:6)
    a. The spirit of the law calls for greater holiness
    b. The law called for Israel to rest on Saturday
    c. Under grace we rest and worship one day a week
    d. For centuries, most Christians have made Sunday that day of rest and worship
5. Ignatius of Antioch said in A.D. 110: "Those who walked in the ancient practices attain unto newness of hope, no longer observing Sabbaths, but fashioning their lives after the Lord's Day, on which our life also rose through Him, that we may be found disciples of Jesus Christ, our only teacher."

III. Conclusion
A. *Keeping a Certain Day of Worship Does Not Save (Rom. 14:5)*
B. *Growth in Grace Comes Through Public and Private Worship*
1. We ought to have private worship every day
2. Sunday is a fitting day for public worship (Col. 2:16–17)

Elizabeth:
The Mother Who Lived on Higher Ground

Mother's Day   *Luke 1:39–40*

I. Introduction

A. *Mary Went to the Hill Country to Visit Her Cousin Elizabeth*
   1. The angel Gabriel had visited Mary
   2. Gabriel had told her of the coming miracle of the birth of Christ
   3. Two faithful women—Mary and Elizabeth—shared a retreat on higher ground

B. *Elizabeth Seems to Have Lived Her Life on Higher Ground*
   1. She and her husband walked with the Lord (1:5–6)
   2. She uttered no complaints even though she was childless

C. *What Kind of a Woman Was Elizabeth?*

II. Body

A. *She Was a Woman of Prayer (v. 6)*
   1. She was righteous before God
      a. Good works cannot make us righteous (Titus 3:5)
      b. We become righteous by faith (Rom. 4:1–5; 10:1–4)
      c. She was, then, a woman of faith
   2. Faith and prayer go hand in hand
   3. Elizabeth and Zacharias had been praying for a son (v. 13)
   4. Praying mothers have accomplished great things
      a. Moses' mother instilled faith in him
      b. The faith of a mother delivered her demon-possessed daughter (Matt. 15:21–28)
      c. Lois and Eunice taught Timothy the Word (2 Tim. 1:5)

B. *She Was a Woman of Patience (vv. 24–25)*
   1. Elizabeth went into hiding for five months
      a. Some women would have made their announcement immediately

        b.   But Elizabeth wanted time alone to rejoice and praise God
- 2. Public rejoicing could wait
  - a. She was on God's timetable
  - b. Another great miracle was in the making
- 3. Carrying a child is a time of waiting that demands patience
- 4. The patience of praying mothers has changed many lives
  - a. How long has your mother waited and prayed for you to trust Christ?
  - b. Don't keep her waiting any longer

C. *She Was a Woman Who Provoked Great Things in Others (vv. 41–79)*
- 1. Mary arrived, and Elizabeth rejoiced
  - a. "Blessed art thou among women"
  - b. "Blessed is the fruit of thy womb"
  - c. Elizabeth saw Mary's child as superior to her own
- 2. Mary was moved to utter the Magnificat (vv. 46–55)
- 3. Elizabeth bore a son and named him John
  - a. Zacharias could speak again
  - b. He broke into the Benedictus (vv. 67–79)

III. Conclusion
A. *Praise God for Praying, Patient Mothers*
B. *Praise God for Mothers Who Provoke Others to Greatness*

The Mother Who Gave Her Son to God

Mother's Day   *1 Samuel 1–2*

I. **Introduction**
  A. *Hannah Was a Woman with a Burden and a Dream*
    1. Hannah was the childless wife of Elkanah
      a. Peninnah, Elkanah's other wife, had children
      b. Peninnah mocked Hannah because she was barren (1:6)
    2. Elkanah loved Hannah, but she still felt unfulfilled
  B. *Hannah Had a Life-Changing Day at the Temple*
    1. Hannah went with her husband to the temple
    2. She went home knowing that she would bear a child
  C. *What Kind of a Woman Was This Miracle Mother?*

II. **Body**
  A. *She Was a Woman Who Kept on Praying (1:10–17)*
    1. Hannah had prayed long for a child without receiving an answer
      a. Years passed, and she was still barren
      b. Tears flowed, and still she had no child
    2. Persistence in prayer is valuable (v. 10)
      a. She prayed when she was feeling down
      b. She prayed until her tears became liquid prayers
    3. Hannah prayed unselfishly and fervently (vv. 11–17)
      a. She promised to give her son to the Lord
      b. Eli was so moved by her praying that he promised her a son
  B. *She Was a Woman Who Kept Her Promises (1:18–28)*
    1. Hannah stopped weeping and started worshiping (vv. 18–19)
    2. The miracle: Samuel was born in answer to her prayer
      a. Hannah chose not to go to the temple until Samuel was weaned
      b. She went later to do important business with God

    3. Two great events occurred in Hannah's life when she went to the temple
        a. She testified of answered prayer: "For this child I prayed"
        b. She gave Samuel to the Lord for life (v. 28)
    4. Keeping our promises to God is important
    5. We must not forget our part when God comes through for us

C. *She Was a Woman Who Kept on Praising (2:1–10)*
    1. "Prayer and praise are happy companions" (C. H. Spurgeon)
    2. Hannah praised the Lord for several reasons
        a. She praised the Lord for His salvation (v. 1)
        b. She praised the Lord for His holiness (v. 2)
        c. She praised the Lord for His faithfulness (v. 2)
        d. She praised the Lord for His power (vv. 5–6)
        e. She praised the Lord for His compassion (vv. 7–9)
        f. She praised the Lord for His present and future victories (v. 10)
    3. Hannah's words still move others to praise Her Lord

III. Conclusion
    A. *We Need Praying, Promise-Keeping, Praising Mothers*
    B. *Children of Mothers Like Hannah Are Fortunate Indeed*

The Past, Present, and Future of Every Christian

Ephesians 2:1–7

I. **Introduction**
  A. *Three Communion Looks*
   1. We look backward to remember Christ's death for us
   2. We look inward to face up to what's within us
   3. We look forward to the Lord's return for us
  B. *Three Other Important Looks*
   1. We need to look to the past to be humble
   2. We need to look to the present to be grateful
   3. We need to look to the future to be joyful

II. **Body**
  A. *The Past of Every Christian (vv. 1–3)*
   1. We don't see a pleasant picture when we look back honestly
   2. We were all dead in trespasses and sins
   3. We all walked according to the course of this sinful world (1 John 2:15–17)
     a. We were living to get (the lust of the flesh)
     b. We were living to gaze (the lust of the eyes)
     c. We were living to gloat (the pride of life)
   4. We were overcome by Satan ("the prince of the power of the air")
     a. Our lives were centered in lust
     b. Our minds were captivated by greed
   5. We deserved the wrath of God (John 3:36)
  B. *The Present of Every Christian (vv. 4–6)*
   1. We have the blessed "but" of salvation: "But God"
     a. But God is rich in mercy
     b. God is rich in everything having to do with salvation
     c. His love enters our lives and changes them
   2. We were dead, but He has made us alive (vv. 5–6)
     a. We were dead in trespasses and sins
     b. Now we are alive in Christ
     c. This new life is the result of His grace

   3. We are seated in heavenly places with Christ
      a. This is made possible by His death for us on
         the cross
      b. We who were far off are made near by His
         grace
C. *The Future of Every Christian (v. 7)*
   1. The best is yet to come
   2. The future ages hold great blessings for believers
      in Christ
      a. Demonstrations of the riches of God's grace to
         us
      b. Experiences that prove His kindness to us
   3. The grace of God was not used up in salvation
      a. This was just the beginning of His many
         kindnesses
      b. No wonder grace will be our song for endless
         ages

III. Conclusion
   A. *Our Past, Present, and Future Should Motivate Us to
      Serve Christ*
   B. *What Are You Doing for This Wonderful Savior Right
      Now?*

Good Work

Philippians 1:6

I. Introduction
  A. *Remembering the Day of Your Conversion*
    1. "Oh happy day that fixed my choice . . ."
    2. Do you remember when you were born again?
  B. *The Christian Life Is More Than Getting Religion*
    1. Baptism and church membership cannot save
    2. Religious ceremonies and pronouncements cannot save
  C. *What Has God Done in Your Life?*

II. Body
  A. *God's Work in You Had a Beginning*
    1. "He who hath begun a good work in you"
    2. You have not always been a Christian
    3. Even so, you have been the beneficiary of God's blessings
      a. The rain falls on the just and the unjust
      b. We are all surrounded by God's handiwork and wonders
    4. Believers have had a special work of God in them
      a. A work of God's Spirit that brought conviction of sin
      b. A work of God that enabled them to understand the gospel
      c. A work of God that brought them to faith in Christ
    5. Has there been a new beginning in your life?
    6. The new birth is absolutely necessary to enter heaven (John 3:1–5)
  B. *God's Work in You Is a Good Work*
    1. "A good work in you"
    2. Some people are afraid to let God work in them
      a. They fear that He might embarrass them
      b. They fear that He might take something away from them
      c. They fear that they might become religious fanatics

   3. But God works for our good
    a. Salvation is a good work
    b. Discipleship is a good work
    c. Personal revival is a good work
   4. God works is us through three things
    a. The Bible (Heb. 4:12)
    b. His Spirit (John 14)
    c. Circumstances (Rom. 8:28)
  C. *God's Work in You Is a Continuing Work*
   1. He "will perform it until the day of Jesus Christ"
   2. God is not through with you yet
   3. The work of God is a permanent work
   4. The goal of God's work is to make you more like Jesus (Rom. 8:28–29)
   5. What does God need to do in you to accomplish His purpose?

III. Conclusion
  A. *Recognize God's Work in You, and Cooperate with Him*
  B. *Respond to God's Work in You Today*

Memorial Stones

Memorial Day   *Joshua 4*

I. **Introduction**
   A. *What Makes Memorial Day Memorable to You?*
      1. Remembering family trips to decorate graves?
      2. Reading epitaphs on memorial stones?
   B. *When God Called for Memorial Stones*
      1. Stones to be taken from the Jordan River
      2. Stones to be placed in the Jordan River

II. **Body**
   A. *Stones to Remember Those Who Gave Their Lives (4:1–3)*
      1. Israel must cross Jordan to enter the Promised Land
         a. Jordan was at flood tide
         b. Crossing then seemed impossible
      2. God's instruction to Joshua was strange (3:13–16)
         a. The priests were to walk into the water
         b. At that moment, Jordan would divide
      3. The priests, in principle, gave their lives
         a. The first step could have led to their drowning
         b. Instead, it delivered them and all Israel
      4. Many people have given their lives for freedom
         a. This fact is true even if they survived the war
         b. We ought to remember them
   B. *Stones to Remember a Great Miracle (vv. 4–8)*
      1. The flooded Jordan opened before the people
         a. Waters piled high upstream (3:16)
         b. Reminiscent of the opening of the Red Sea
      2. Communion and baptism are memorials to a great miracle
         a. Christ died and rose again
         b. This was the greatest miracle of the ages
      3. The Israelites took stones from the Jordan River to carry on their journey
         a. We have a mission for our journey
         b. We are to carry the message of Christ's death and resurrection

   C. *Stones to Remember Crossing Jordan Safely (4:9–24)*
1. All Israel passed over on dry ground (3:17)
2. They placed the stones in Jordan as memorials of this miracle
3. The flooded Jordan is a symbol of death
   a. Death comes to all (Heb. 9:27)
   b. Even all believers must cross this river
   c. But we don't have to cross Jordan alone (Ps. 23:4)
   d. Christ's resurrection proves that we'll cross Jordan safely (1 Cor. 15:20)
4. No wonder we find comfort when loved ones die (1 Thess. 4:13–18)!

III. Conclusion
   A. *Memorial Stones Remind Us That Life Is Short*
   B. *Faith in Christ Prepares Us for Heaven*
   C. *Will Others Remember That You Crossed Jordan Safely?*

Life's Last Beatitude

Revelation 14:13

I. **Introduction**
   A. *We're Familiar with the Beatitudes of Jesus*
      1. Here is a beatitude spoken by an unknown voice from heaven
      2. It is a beatitude of comfort for all who lose loved ones in death
   B. *This Is a Beatitude for the End of a Believer's Life*
      1. "Blessed are the dead." Can this be true?
      2. The key to this mystery is that these people died in the Lord
   C. *What Blessings Do Believers Who Die Receive?*

II. **Body**
   A. *The Blessing of Rest*
      1. "That they may rest from their labors"
      2. The setting of this beatitude is the Tribulation period on earth
         a. One hundred forty-four believers followed the Lamb (vv. 1–5)
         b. These people were preachers of the gospel (v. 6)
         c. They had undergone great persecution, even martyrdom
         d. Now they had found rest with their Lord
      3. Many people are weary from long years of labor
      4. Some people are weary from enduring hard trials
      5. Others are weary from years of sickness
      6. Old soldiers may be weary from fighting for freedom
      7. Heaven will bring long-awaited rest
   B. *The Blessing of Rewards*
      1. "Their works do follow them"
      2. We are not saved by works (Eph. 2:8–10)
         a. We are saved by grace through faith
         b. But the saved are His workmanship, created to do good works
      3. The believer's good works bring rewards in heaven

        a. Rewards for enduring persecution for Christ (Matt. 5:12)

        b. Rewards for loving enemies and doing good (Luke 6:35)

        c. Rewards for faithful service (1 Cor. 3:8–14)

        d. Rewards for serving willingly (1 Cor. 9:17)

    4. The faithful few who serve so well now will be rewarded then

C. *The Blessing of Reunion*

    1. The saved will be reunited with believing loved ones

        a. Heaven is a place of reunion

        b. We will know our loved ones in heaven

    2. Our Lord offered comforting words to His disciples (John 14:1–3)

        a. They were not to be troubled by His coming death

        b. He was going to prepare a place for them

        c. They would meet Him in heaven and be with Him forever

    3. We'll enjoy the "no mores" of heaven: no more death, sorrow, crying, or pain (Rev. 21:4)

III. Conclusion

A. *Every Believer Dies with a Beatitude*

B. *We Can Be Sure That the Best Is Yet to Come (Rom. 8:18)*

Daniel:
The Man Who Learned God's Secrets

Series on the Future Begins   *Daniel 1:1–20*

I. **Introduction**
   A. *Daniel's Amazing Book*
      1. A book of adventures in faith
      2. A book that previews the future
   B. *Daniel's Amazing Life*
      1. Taken captive from Judah to Babylon
      2. Chosen as one of four to serve Nebuchadnezzar
      3. Shown God's plan for the future
   C. *Why God Shared His Secrets with Daniel*

II. **Body**
   A. *Daniel's Clean Heart (v. 8)*
      1. "Daniel purposed in his heart"
         a. Influenced Shadrach, Meshach, and Abednego
         b. Purposed to keep their hearts clean for the Lord
      2. Daniel's decision required faith and courage
         a. "The secret of the Lord is with them that fear Him" (Ps. 25:14)
         b. God reveals His secrets to those who trust Him
      3. David also came to desire a clean heart (Ps. 51:10)
      4. Daniel's decision affected his choices in life
         a. He would refuse the king's wine and meat
         b. He would live differently than his captors
   B. *Daniel's Consistent Life (vv. 8–10)*
      1. It is not far from resolution to reality
         a. Testing is sure to follow testimony
         b. Melzar arrived with the king's meat and wine
      2. Daniel requested to be excused from taking this food and drink
         a. He respectfully stated his convictions
         b. His consistent life affected Melzar and moved him to agree
      3. Daniel's example of courage and faith overcame Melzar's fears

    C. *Daniel's Confidence in God (vv. 11–16)*
1. The test of faith: "Prove thy servants"
2. Living lean in a land of plenty
   a. Vegetable soup tasted better than wine and meat
   b. Obedience to God makes life sweet
3. Results of this test of faith and obedience
   a. Daniel and his friends were healthier than the others
   b. Even the unbelievers saw the difference

III. Conclusion
    A. *Those Who Live Close to God Learn His Secrets*
1. God gave these four faithful young men knowledge, skill in learning, and wisdom
2. Daniel was given an understanding of the secrets of God
3. Spurgeon: "Saints can understand heavenly mysteries. They have been initiated into the fellowship of the skies."
    B. *How Close to God Are You?*

Daniel Views the Future

I. Introduction

A. *The "ABC" Chapter for the Study of Prophecy*
   1. A basic chapter to understand God's prophetic plan
   2. Tracing a path through the centuries from the captivity to the kingdom

B. *Foundational Facts of the Chapter*
   1. Daniel and three friends are captives in Babylon
   2. Nebuchadnezzar, the king, had a prophetic dream
   3. The king's dilemma was that he couldn't remember his dream
      a. He demanded that his advisers tell him what his dream meant (v. 5)
      b. Execution was ahead because they could not do so (v. 11)
   4. Facing death, Daniel and his friends went to prayer (vv. 14–18)
      a. They knew where to turn in a crisis
      b. It is always better to pray than to panic

II. Body

A. *Daniel's Information About the Kingdoms of Earth (vv. 19–43)*
   1. The king's dream revealed to Daniel (v. 19)
      a. Daniel praised God for this revelation (vv. 19–22)
      b. Daniel gave thanks for answered prayer (v. 23)
      c. Daniel testified to Nebuchadnezzar (vv. 24–30)
   2. The image of gold, silver, brass, iron, and iron mixed with clay (vv. 32–33)
   3. Daniel's interpretation of the king's dream (vv. 36–45)
      a. The head of gold: Nebuchadnezzar and his kingdom
      b. The breast and arms of silver: the Medo-Persian Empire
      c. The belly and thighs of brass: the Grecian Empire

95

   d. The legs of iron: the Roman Empire

   e. The feet of iron and clay: the Roman Empire's final form

  4. The stone that fell on the iron and clay: Christ's Kingdom

 B. *Daniel's Insights About the Kingdom of Christ (vv. 44–45)*

  1. Christ is the stone cut without hands (Ps. 118:22)

  2. The European union (the revived Roman Empire) is a sign of the last days

  3. John and Daniel agree (Rev. 13:1; 17:12–18)

  4. The stone will break the iron and clay to pieces (v. 34)

  5. The God of heaven will set up His kingdom (vv. 44–45)

   a. Christ will be king (Rev. 19)

   b. Christ's kingdom will never be destroyed

 C. *Daniel's Impact on the King of Babylon (vv. 46–49)*

  1. Nebuchadnezzar's mistake: he worshiped Daniel

  2. The king's correct conclusion

   a. Daniel's God is above all

   b. He is a God of gods, a Lord of kings, a revealer of secrets

  3. The king made Daniel a ruler over the province of Babylon

III. Conclusion

 A. *The King Is Coming. Are You Ready?*

 B. *Do You Know This Eternal King as Your Savior and Lord?*

The Empires of Earth and Eternity

Series on the Future   *Daniel 7*

I. **Introduction**
   A. *Daniel: The Book of Revelation in the Old Testament*
      1. Necessary to understand prophecy
      2. So accurate in fulfillment that critics cannot explain it
   B. *The Dream of the Interpreter of Dreams*
      1. Nebuchadnezzar's dream is interpreted in chapter 2
      2. Now Daniel has a dream of his own to interpret
   C. *Daniel's Dream and Its Interpretation*

II. **Body**
   A. *The Empires (vv. 1–7)*
      1. Daniel has a dream about animals
      2. Daniel's dream is related to the dream of Nebuchadnezzar
         a. Nebuchadnezzar's dream views the empires from earth's perspective
         b. Daniel's dream views the empires as God sees them
      3. The lion represents the Babylonian Empire
         a. It is first as strong as a lion but then as weak as a man
         b. See Nebuchadnezzar's humbling in Daniel 4
      4. The bear represents the Medo-Persian Empire
         a. Raised on one side: the Persians were stronger
         b. Three ribs: the three chief Babylonian cities
      5. The leopard represents the Grecian Empire
         a. Alexander the Great conquered with lightning speed
         b. In the end, the empire was controlled by four generals
      6. The fourth beast represents the Roman Empire
   B. *The End Time (vv. 7–8)*
      1. The fearsome fourth beast had ten horns
         a. In Nebuchadnezzar's dream, the image had ten toes

        b. This is compared to the coming evil empire
          (Rev. 13:1; 17:12)
    2. The little horn was speaking great things: the evil
       one
       a. He will have great power
       b. He will put down three leaders
       c. He will oppose and try to destroy God's people
    3. This evil one will be eloquent and convincing, and
       many people will follow him
       a. All nations will become subservient to him
       b. True believers will resist him and suffer
         persecution

  C. *The Eternal Kingdom (vv. 9–14)*
    1. All earthly thrones will finally be overthrown
    2. Christ, the Ancient of Days, will come to reign
    3. The kingdom will be given to the saints (v. 27)
    4. This kingdom will last forever (vv. 9, 14)

III. Conclusion
  A. *We've Studied a Preview of the Drama of the Ages*
  B. *We've Seen a Clear Picture of the Coming Final*
    Conflict
  C. *Who Is on the Lord's Side Today?*

The Time of the End

Series on the Future   *Daniel 12*

I. **Introduction**
   A. *Tough Times Ahead (v. 1)*
      1. Looking ahead, Daniel sees the Tribulation
      2. This will be Earth's most terrible time (Matt. 24:21)
   B. *Revelations Concerning the Resurrection*
      1. Some rise to everlasting life
      2. Some rise to shame and everlasting contempt
      3. Soul winners rise to receive eternal rewards
   C. *What Will the End Time Be?*

II. **Body**
   A. *A Busy Time (v. 4)*
      1. "Many shall run to and fro"
         a. This is a commentary on our time
         b. Everyone is on the move
      2. Busy schedules dominate families
      3. Speed and ease of travel are unprecedented
         a. Crowded highways are the norm everywhere
         b. Thousands of people are frequent fliers
         c. Contrast our time of speed and travel with any other period in history
      4. Sadly, many of us are too busy to take time for God
      5. Are you too busy to take time for God?
   B. *A Brilliant Time (v. 4)*
      1. "Knowledge shall be increased"
      2. The amount of knowledge will explode at the end time
         a. An increase in scientific knowledge
         b. An increase in medical knowledge
         c. An increase in technical knowledge
      3. Now we have "artificial knowledge"
         a. The computer age with all its wonders
         b. Affects all areas of life and fulfills prophecy
      4. New communication breakthroughs continue to change our lives

      5. Since knowledge multiplies, acceleration of knowledge will increase
- C. *A Blind Time (v. 10)*
  1. "None of the wicked shall understand"
  2. Increased wickedness in spite of increased enlightenment
     - a. "The wicked do wickedly"
     - b. Education doesn't improve morality
  3. Compare to Paul's description of this time (2 Tim. 3)
  4. "Ever learning, and never able to come to the knowledge of the truth"

III. Conclusion
- A. *The Blessed Ones at the Time of the End*
  1. They are purified (1 John 2:3)
  2. "The wise shall understand"
- B. *Blessings or Spiritual Blindness: Which Will It Be?*

Prophetic Lessons in a Cemetery

Series on the Future   *Ezekiel 37:1–14*

I. **Introduction**
   A. *Ezekiel's Strange Vision*
      1. A trip to the cemetery reveals a valley of human bones
      2. The bones come together
      3. They have flesh but no breath in them
      4. Finally breath comes, and they become an army
   B. *The Meaning of the Vision*
      1. The bones represent Israel (v. 11)
      2. The graves are the nations to which Israel has been scattered
      3. The moving of the bones is their return to their land
      4. Breath and life speak of their future conversion to Christ
   C. *The Life Principles in This Prophetic Picture*

II. **Body**
   A. *Sin Brings Chastening and Judgment (vv. 1–3)*
      1. Moses prophesied Israel's future
         a. Blessings for obedience (Deut. 28:1–4)
         b. Chastening for disobedience (Deut. 28:15–68)
      2. The people chose to disobey, and trouble followed
         a. Captivity by the Assyrians
         b. Captivity by the Babylonians
      3. A remnant returned under Ezra and Nehemiah
         a. A temporary revival took place
         b. Disobedience returned, and discipline came again
      4. The Romans conquered and oppressed them
      5. Christ came and was rejected and crucified
      6. Centuries of persecution followed
   B. *God Speaks to the Troubled and the Oppressed (vv. 4–6)*
      1. "Prophesy unto these bones"
         a. This was a strange command
         b. God still speaks to those who are dead in sin
      2. "I will cause breath to enter into you"

101

       3. Our Lord calls to those whom we think are beyond hope
         a. "Come now and let us reason together" (Isa. 1:18)
         b. "Come unto me all ye that labor" (Matt. 11:28)
       4. God calls to the lost and the backslidden
       5. Have you responded to His call?

    C. *God Meets Us Where We Are and Gives Us Life (vv. 7–14)*
       1. The bones come together and gain flesh but no breath
       2. Breath and life arrive, and a great army is born
       3. The return of Israel to their land is a prophetic miracle
       4. A future day will bring conversion, breath, and life

III. Conclusion
    A. *Christ Brings Life to Those Who Are Dead in Sin (John 11:25)*
    B. *Trust in Christ, and Come Alive!*

How Near Closing Time?

Series on the Future   *Matthew 24*

I. Introduction
   A. *Those Curious Disciples (v. 3)*
      1. "What shall be the sign of thy coming?"
      2. Many people have repeated this question through the centuries
   B. *Jesus Answering the Question of the Ages*
      1. This chapter gives signs of Christ's return
      2. Do they describe conditions in our time?

II. Body
   A. *Wars and Rumors of Wars (vv. 6–7)*
      1. Wars have been evident throughout history
      2. In our time, however, war is far more deadly
         a. Weapons of immense power to maim and kill
         b. Weapons that reach across continents in minutes
      3. Paul adds the "peace" dimension to this prophecy
         a. Peace to seem almost within our grasp
         b. The passion for peace in the Middle East
         c. Success for lasting peace to seem promising
         d. Then . . . sudden destruction (1 Thess. 5:1–3)
   B. *The Travail of Nature (v. 7)*
      1. Famines brought by floods and drought
      2. Pestilence (diseases) from disasters
         a. Storms that make medical treatment difficult
         b. Breeding places for multiplying bacteria
      3. Earthquakes increasing steadily and becoming more violent
   C. *Signs in the Nations (vv. 32–35)*
      1. The sign of Israel now a nation (the fig tree)
      2. And "all the trees" (Luke 21:29)
      3. European union (the revived Roman Empire)
      4. China's growing military capability (Rev. 9:13–21)
      5. The Middle East as the powder keg of the world
   D. *The Sign of Increased Iniquity (vv. 36–39)*
      1. Conditions to be like those in Noah's time
         a. People living for the pleasure of the moment

103

  b. Alcohol and drug use rampant
  c. Violence increasing everywhere
 2. Conditions also to be like those in Sodom
  a. Immorality on the increase
  b. Perversion accepted as normal

III. **Conclusion**
 A. *Do You See These Signs on the Rise Today?*
 B. *What Are You Doing to Prepare for Closing Time?*
  1. Have you received Christ as your Savior?
  2. Are you living daily in His will?
  3. Are you seizing opportunities to tell others of Him?

Armageddon

Series on the Future   *Revelation 16:15*

I. Introduction
   A. *The Meaning of Armageddon*
   1. Has come to stand for the most terrible of wars
   2. Means "Mount of Megiddo," a hill overlooking a battlefield
   3. A favorite battlefield throughout history
   B. *Timeline to Armageddon*
   1. The rapture of the church (1 Cor. 15:51)
   2. The revealing of the Antichrist (2 Thess. 2:7–10)
   3. Armageddon at the end of the Tribulation (Dan. 9:27)

II. Body
   A. *Certainties About Armageddon*
   1. Involves all of the nations (Joel 3:12)
   2. Pits all of the nations against the Lord (Ps. 2)
   3. Ends with the coming of Christ as King of kings (Rev. 19:11)
   B. *Events Leading to Armageddon*
   1. A seven-year peace treaty is arranged for Israel (Dan. 9:26–27)
   2. The Antichrist breaks this treaty in mid-duration (Dan. 9:26–27)
   3. One hundred forty-four Jews are converted and begin to minister (Rev. 7)
   4. God's two witnesses minister and are martyred (Rev. 11)
      a. Who are these witnesses? Probably Enoch and Elijah
      b. Enoch will preach his old message again (Jude 14–15)
      c. These prophets declare the Lord's imminent return to reign
      d. They may even reveal how much time remains
   5. The Antichrist summons earth's armies to Armageddon

      a. They are to fight against Christ at His coming (Ps. 2)
      b. This is to be all-out war against God (Joel 3:9–14)
  6. Man's ultimate rebellion takes place
      a. "We will not have this man rule over us"
      b. Sinful men foolishly think hi-tech weapons will prevail

C. *The End of Armageddon (Rev. 19:17–21)*
  1. Christ returns in power and great glory
  2. He is declared to be King of kings and Lord of lords
  3. The Antichrist and his armies are defeated
  4. The deceivers are destroyed
      a. The beast and the false prophets are exposed as frauds
      b. They are cast into the lake of fire

III. Conclusion
A. *Have You Been Rebelling Against God?*
B. *Turn Away from the One Who Has Deceived You*
C. *Turn to Christ While There Is Still Time*
  1. We are in the countdown stage of history
  2. Signs of the Lord's return are everywhere
  3. Our Lord will come when we do not expect Him
  4. Don't delay for even one more day getting right with Him

The King Is Coming

Series on the Future   *Revelation 19:11–21*

I. **Introduction**
   A. *Great Things Ahead for Believers*
      1. The rapture of the church (1 Thess. 4:13–18)
      2. The rewards received in heaven (Rev. 22:12)
      3. The marriage supper of the Lamb (Rev. 19:7–9)
   B. *Preparing for Another Triumphal Entry*
      1. The first when Jesus rode into Jerusalem on a colt (Luke 19:30–48)
      2. The next when Jesus rides in on a white horse (Rev. 19:11)
      3. The preview that John gives of that exciting ride

II. **Body**
   A. *The King's Arrival (vv. 11–13)*
      1. After the supper, the King rises and leaves
         a. Time to depart heaven for earth
         b. He must return to earth as He promised (John 14:1–3)
      2. What's been happening on earth?
         a. Earth's most terrible time, the tribulation (Matt. 24:21)
         b. Satanic deception, disease, and destruction
      3. The King arrives riding on a white horse
      4. The King has several names
         a. Faithful and true (v. 11)
         b. A secret name (v. 12)
         c. The Word of God (v. 13)
      5. The King's eyes are as a flame of fire: judgment (v. 12)
      6. The King's vesture is dipped in blood: the cross (v. 13)
   B. *The King's Armies (v. 14)*
      1. Those who had joined Him in heaven
      2. Those cleansed by the blood of the Lamb (Rev. 5:9)
      3. An army clothed in fine, white, clean linen

107

          a.   This army once wore filthy rags (Isa. 64:6)
          b.   These clean robes were furnished by their
              King
     4.   The army riding on white horses, like the King
     5.   This army to rule and reign with the King

C. *The King's Anger (vv. 15–21)*
     1.   He rebukes the nations with His Word
     2.   He will rule them with a rod of iron
     3.   He ends the battle of Armageddon (vv. 17–18)
     4.   He casts the beast and the false prophet into the
        lake of fire (v. 20)
     5.   He and His army get complete victory through His
        Word (v. 21)

III. **Conclusion**
   A. *Christ Is Revealed as the King of Kings and Lord of
      Lords*
   B. *Is Christ the King and Lord of Your Life?*
     1.   Stop resisting the King
     2.   Surrender completely to the King
     3.   Let the victorious King change all of your defeats
        to victories

Righteousness or Reproach?

Independence Day   *Proverbs 14:34*

I. **Introduction**
   A. *A Day for Celebrating Freedom*
      1. The courage of those who dared to proclaim liberty
      2. Liberty, a cherished biblical principle (Lev. 25:10)
   B. *How to Secure the Blessings of Liberty for the Future*
      1. Solomon's good advice for any nation
      2. A national choice between righteousness and reproach
   C. *Three Important Questions for Us All*

II. **Body**
   A. *What Builds Up a Nation?*
      1. "Righteousness exalteth a nation"
      2. Political leaders usually prescribe the following:
         a. A mighty military force
         b. A strong economy and the development of resources
         c. Improvement of education and technology
      3. Righteousness is a nation's greatest treasure
      4. Righteous living determines a nation's destiny (Deut. 28–30)
      5. Charles Bridges's Proverbs commentary on this text: "The history of the chosen people, as they were a righteous or sinful nation, is marked by corresponding exaltation or disgrace."
   B. *What Brings Down a Nation?*
      1. "Sin is a reproach to any people"
      2. Consider the decline of a civilization in Romans 1
         a. They refused to glorify God and be thankful
         b. They chose idolatry over true worship
         c. They practiced many forms of immorality
         d. They became violent, deceitful, and proud
      3. Sin brought the downfall of many once-proud empires
         a. The Babylonian Empire (Belshazzer's death: Dan. 5)
         b. The Medo-Persian and Grecian empires
         c. The Roman Empire

    4. Neither nations nor individuals can sin and win (Num. 32:23)

C. *Who Makes the Difference?*
   1. Bridges: "What an enemy ungodly man is to his country!"
   2. National exaltation depends on how individual citizens live
      a. A nation is blessed by righteous citizens
      b. A nation is disgraced by unrighteous citizens
   3. Righteousness is not legislated but lived out by individuals
   4. How we live makes a difference for the future of our country

III. **Conclusion**
   A. *A Call to Personal Holiness*
   B. *A Call to Search Our Hearts*
   C. *A Call for Confession of Sin and Full Surrender (1 John 1:9)*

No More Bombs Bursting in Air

Series on the Future Ends

1 Thessalonians 5:1–4;
Micah 4:1–5

I. **Introduction**
   A. *Freedom Has Been Purchased with Blood*
     1. Liberty has always come through the overthrow of tyrants
     2. Wars have drenched battlefields with blood to gain freedom
   B. *Wars Have Been Fought to End All Wars*
     1. Still the world is an armed camp, a dangerous place
     2. Wars and rumors of war will continue (Matt. 24:6–7)
   C. *When Will the World Find Peace?*

II. **Body**
   A. *Peace Is the Cry of the Earth Today (1 Thess. 5:1–4)*
     1. People have longed for peace throughout the centuries
       a. Even so, war has continued to plague the earth
       b. No wonder the cry for peace has continued
     2. Why wars continue (James 4:1–4)
       a. Lust for power and property
       b. The desire to control wealth and people
     3. Peace will finally seem within the grasp of mankind
       a. People will believe that peace and safety has arrived
       b. Even then, destruction will be on its way
     4. Believers are to be alert to these signs of Christ's return
     5. These are days to watch and pray
   B. *Peace Is Coming to the Earth Someday (Mark 4:1–2)*
     1. A time of religious peace (v. 1)
     2. A time of political peace (v. 2)
     3. A time of peace through justice (Isa. 11:1–5)
     4. A time of peace in nature (Isa. 11:6–8; 35:1–2)
       a. The enmity between animals will end

       b. The enmity between people and animals will end
       c. The earth will produce abundantly
   5. A time when violence will end (Isa. 11:9)
       a. Violence has been with us since the Fall
       b. There will be no hurting or destroying in that coming time of peace

C. *Peace Will Come When the King Comes Again (Mark 4:3–4)*
   1. Peace agreements will fail until the Prince of Peace returns (Isa. 9:6–7)
   2. Christ will judge among the people
       a. He will rebuke the wicked
       b. He will bring fairness to all
   3. Christ will end all war
       a. Weapons will be put to better use
       b. "Neither shall they learn war anymore"

III. Conclusion
   A. *We Can Find Peace with God Now by Faith (Rom. 5:1)*
   B. *We Can Have Personal Peace by Full Surrender (Phil. 4:6–8)*

Fixing a Troubled Church

Revelation 2:12–17

I. **Introduction**
   A. *Seven Letters from Jesus*
      1. Letters to seven churches
      2. Each letter addressing special needs
   B. *Jesus' Message to a Compromising Church*
      1. Presents Himself as the one to cure their ills
      2. His remedy: the sharp, two-edged sword—the Bible (Heb. 4:12)
   C. *Encouragement and Advice for the Church at Pergamos*

II. **Body**
   A. *Where the Church Was Faithful (vv. 12–13)*
      1. Jesus encouraged before offering advise
         a. A good example for us all
         b. Christlike to first point out the positive (Phil. 4:8)
      2. Pergamos was a tough place to be faithful
         a. The location of "Satan's seat"
         b. A center of Asian idolatry
      3. The church at Pergamos was faithful to the Lord's name
      4. The church at Pergamos had not denied the faith
         a. Faithful even under persecution
         b. Faithful Antipas was martyred
      5. Would we have been faithful in those circumstances?
   B. *Where the Church Was Faltering (vv. 14–15)*
      1. The church had embraced two serious errors
         a. The doctrine of Baalam (Num. 22)
            (1) Knew God's will but didn't do it
            (2) Encouraged compromise with unbelievers (2 Cor. 6:17–18)
            (3) Tolerated immorality among believers
         b. The doctrine of the Nicolaitanes
            (1) From deeds in Ephesus (2:6) to doctrine here
            (2) Leaders lording it over other believers
            (3) Sacrificing the priesthood of the believer

113

  2. These dangerous doctrines placed the church in jeopardy

 C. *Where the Church Was Faulty (v. 16)*

  1. The church at Pergamos needed to repent

   a. To repent is to turn around, to do an *about face!*

   b. Does our church need to repent?

  2. The church also needed to return to God's Word

   a. "I will fight . . . with the sword of my mouth" (Heb. 4:12)

   b. Programs cannot compare with the power of God's Word

  3. Repentance and returning to God's Word brings revival

III. **Conclusion**

 A. *The Lord's Call Becomes Personal: "He that hath an ear" (v. 17)*

 B. *Overcomers Will Get Rewards: A White Stone and a New Name*

 C. *Heaven's Rewards Surpass Our Understanding*

The Poor Rich Church

Revelation 3:14–22

I. Introduction

A. *Dynamic Churches Are the Hope of a Nation*
1. Effective churches bring people to Christ and righteous living
2. Churches on fire for Christ improve the spiritual temperature of a nation

B. *Christ Addresses a Failing Church*
1. The church at Laodicea looked good but lacked spiritual power
2. It was a church that fooled the public but not the Savior

II. Body

A. *The All-Knowing Christ (vv. 14–16)*
1. We learn how Christ introduced Himself to the church
   a. The Amen: Christ is unchangeable
   b. The faithful and true witness: Christ keeps His promises
   c. The beginning of the creation of God: Christ is eternal
2. Christ was not deceived by the appearance of success in this church
   a. He knows what is going on in all of the churches
   b. He sees beyond the buildings and the budgets
3. Christ saw how little passion this church had for God and souls
   a. They were only going through the motions of religion
   b. Inwardly they were lukewarm to eternal truth
4. Christ was disappointed in them and told them so
5. What is the spiritual temperature of our church? Are we a disappointment to Jesus?

B. *The Awesome Needs of This Church (vv. 17–19)*
1. How did the members of the church at Laodicea see themselves?

          a.   They boasted of being rich and increased with goods

          b.   They thought that they needed nothing

   2.   Churches can make tragic trades

          a.   Trading spiritual fire for fineries; prayer for possessions

          b.   Trading power with God for prestige with men

          c.   Trading powerful preaching for partisan politics

   3.   The church appeared to be rich but was spiritually poor

   4.   Jesus recommended the following for this poor rich church

          a.   Gold tried in the fire (faithfulness when enduring persecution)

          b.   White raiment (righteousness produced by faith)

          c.   Eyesalve (spiritual perception gained through Bible study and prayer)

   5.   Jesus warned of rebuke and chastening unless changes were made (v. 19)

  C. *The Affectionate Knocking of the Savior (v. 20)*

     1.   The Lord turns to individuals, knocking on each heart's door

          a.   He does not knock once like opportunity; He keep's knocking

          b.   He does not knock like a salesman, for His own profit

     2.   Christ knocks and calls out to each one, offering to come in

     3.   Opening the door brings eternal life and fellowship with Jesus

III. Conclusion

  A. *Eternal Rewards Are Promised to Those Who Open and Overcome*

  B. *Have You Opened Your Heart's Door to Jesus?*

The Church That Ministered to a Prisoner

Series in Colossians Begins   *Colossians 1:1–8*

I. **Introduction**
   A. *Introducing the Series in Colossians*
      1. One of the richest of Paul's letters
      2. A deep source of truth concerning Christ
   B. *Paul Refreshed and Revived While Writing from Prison*
      1. Epaphras brought news from Colossae that ministered to Paul
      2. Joy filled Paul's heart over what was happening in this church
   C. *What Caused Paul Such Joy Over These Believers?*

II. **Body**
   A. *Their Strong Faith in the Savior (vv. 1–4)*
      1. "To the saints and brethren in Christ"
      2. These believers were genuine
         a. Paul knew that they were real and called them saints
         b. He rejoiced that they were faithful to Christ
      3. Just hearing about these Christians made Paul thankful (v. 3)
      4. He found himself praying for them often
      5. Their strong faith refreshed Paul's soul
         a. Faith evidenced in their prayers
         b. Faith demonstrated in their giving
      6. Spurgeon on faith: "A little faith will bring your soul to heaven; great faith will bring heaven to your soul."
   B. *Their Sincere Love for All Believers (v. 4)*
      1. "The love which ye have to all the saints"
      2. What a great reputation for any church!
      3. Love is the badge of discipleship (John 13:35)
      4. Love proves that we've passed from death to life (1 John 3:14)
      5. Without love, we're nothing (1 Cor. 13:3)
      6. Love for all saints should begin with those closest to us

         a. Active love in our homes
         b. Active love in our churches
     7. Love ends strife and builds fellowship
     8. No wonder Paul was refreshed by this loving church
  C. *Their Sure Hope of Heaven (v. 5)*
     1. "For the hope which is laid up for you in heaven"
     2. Heaven was real to these faithful believers
         a. This world was not their home
         b. They longed and lived for heaven
     3. They were laying up their treasures in heaven
         a. "Which is laid up for you"
         b. A great motivation for Christian service

III. Conclusion
  A. *How Are Others Affected by Our Faith, Hope, and Love?*
  B. *Do We Refresh or Discourage Other Believers?*
  C. *What Can We Do to Minister to Others Every Day?*

How to Pray for Those We Love

Colossians 1:9–11

I. **Introduction**
   A. *Paul's Deep Love for the Colossian Christians*
      1. He felt close to them, even from a distance
      2. He rejoiced in their faith, hope, and love
   B. *Paul Shares His Prayer for Those Whom He Loved*
      1. It's easy to say, "I'll be praying for you"
      2. Paul was specific, telling them how he prayed

II. **Body**
   A. *Paul Prayed That They Would Know God's Will (v. 9)*
      1. "Filled with the knowledge of his will"
      2. See how important this prayer was to Paul
         a. He could have prayed that they would not be persecuted
         b. He could have prayed that they would prosper
         c. He could have prayed that they would gain political power
      3. Knowing God's will was more important than any of these
      4. With what knowledge are you filled?
         a. The knowledge of world conditions?
         b. The knowledge of everything in the world of sports?
         c. The knowledge of how to succeed in business?
         d. The knowledge that brings academic recognition?
      5. Are you filled with the knowledge of God's will?
   B. *Paul Prayed That They Would Know How to Walk (v. 10)*
      1. "That ye might walk worthy of the Lord"
      2. Spiritual understanding teaches how to walk worthy of the Lord
         a. We gain spiritual understanding through prayer
         b. We gain spiritual understanding through Bible study
         c. We gain spiritual understanding through worship

119

      3. What is meant by walking worthy of the Lord?
         a. It is to walk in the Spirit (Gal. 5:16)
         b. It is to walk in love (Eph. 5:2)
         c. It is to walk as children of light (Eph. 5:8)
      4. When we walk worthy of the Lord, others notice
      5. When we walk worthy of the Lord, we become fruitful in His work

C. *Paul Prayed That They Would Know God Well (v. 10)*
      1. "Increasing in the knowledge of God"
         a. Not just in knowing about God
         b. Means knowing God more intimately
      2. This is what Paul was seeking for himself (Phil. 3:7–14)
      3. Knowing God well should be our goal
      4. How well do you know God?

III. Conclusion
    A. *How Do You Pray for Those Whom You Love?*
    B. *Do Your Prayers Center Only on Temporary Things?*
    C. *Let's Pray About How Our Loved Ones Walk with God*

Heirs with the Saints and the King

Series in Colossians   *Colossians 1:12*

I. **Introduction**
  A. *Paul Calls for Thankful People*
     1. He had written about his thankful heart (v. 3)
     2. Now he moves from experience to expectation (v. 12)
  B. *We Are Partakers of the Inheritance of the Saints*
     1. Other uses of "partakers"
        a. Partakers of grace (Phil. 1:7)
        b. Partakers of Christ's sufferings (1 Peter 4:13)
        c. Partakers of the divine nature (2 Peter 1:4)
     2. What it means to be heirs with the saints

II. **Body**
  A. *We Are Heirs of Righteousness (Heb. 11:7)*
     1. Righteousness seems so far from us
        a. We know this from observation (the sins of others)
        b. We know this from experience (our own sins)
     2. Noah lived in a wicked age
        a. He was surrounded by violent sinners
        b. Yet he became an heir of righteousness
     3. Noah's righteousness came by faith
        a. This was also true of Abraham (Rom. 4:3)
        b. Faith makes us heirs of righteousness
  B. *We Are Heirs of the Kingdom (James 2:5)*
     1. The Bible is a book about a kingdom
        a. A spiritual kingdom
        b. A literal, coming kingdom
     2. The poor can become heirs of the kingdom
        a. This is an inheritance of faith
        b. This is an inheritance of those who love Christ
     3. Abraham was called an heir of the world (Rom. 4:13–16)
        a. He did not gain this inheritance through good works
        b. He became an heir of the world through faith
     4. The paradox of the kingdom promise

        a. Those living for this world will not receive it
        b. Those living by faith will inherit all things
  C. *We Are Joint Heirs with Christ (Rom. 8:14–17)*
     1. We became heirs of our parents at our physical birth
     2. We became heirs of God at our second birth (John 1:12; 3:5)
     3. As God's children, we have become joint heirs with Christ
     4. This inheritance has amazing dimensions
        a. What Jesus owns we will own
        b. Where Jesus reigns we will reign

III. Conclusion
  A. *Are You Living Like an Heir of the King?*
  B. *Remember Who You Are, and Rejoice*

Delivered from Darkness

Series in Colossians   *Colossians 1:13–17*

I. Introduction
  A. *Faith in Christ Brings Freedom*
    1. The truth makes us free (John 8:32)
    2. The Son makes us free (John 8:36)
  B. *The Power of Darkness Is an Obstacle to Freedom*
    1. What is the power of darkness?
    2. How is deliverance possible?
    3. Why is our Deliverer able to set us free?

II. Body
  A. *The Power of Darkness (v. 13)*
    1. Darkness speaks of sin
      a. Men love darkness rather than light (John 3:19)
      b. The reason is that their deeds are evil
    2. Sin holds many people in bondage
      a. Sin blinds and intensifies darkness
      b. Wise ones avoid the works of darkness (Eph. 5:11)
    3. The power of sin flows from the rulers of darkness
      a. Believers are in conflict with these rulers (Eph. 6:12)
      b. Our Lord equips us to win this battle (Eph. 6:10–18)
    4. Christ, the Light, overcomes the power of darkness
    5. Those who walk with Christ have the light of life (John 8:12)
  B. *The Possibility of Deliverance (v. 14)*
    1. "In whom we have redemption through his blood"
      a. We have been redeemed (bought back)
      b. What good news!
    2. Deliverance from bondage calls for praise
      a. Moses leading his people from slavery in Egypt
      b. Israel's song of deliverance (Exod. 15)
    3. Our deliverance includes the forgiveness of sins
      a. The old account is settled

           b.   Nothing can be brought up against the redeemed

      4.   The promise of deliverance was given in Eden (Gen. 3:15)

      5.   The payment for deliverance was paid at Calvary (1 Peter 1:18–19)

  C. *The Perfect Deliverer (vv. 15–17)*

      1.   "The image of the invisible God"

           a.   "All things were made by him" (John 1:3)

           b.   Scofield: "Christ, as the eternal Son, holds the priority."

      2.   Christ created all principalities and powers (v. 16)

           a.   He is, then, far above them (Eph. 1:21)

           b.   He has triumphed over them (Col. 2:15)

      3.   The power of darkness cannot stand against Him

III.   Conclusion

  A. *In Christ Our Deliverance Is Sure*

  B. *Rest Your Faith in This Perfect Deliverer*

The Head of the Church

Series in Colossians   *Colossians 1:18–22*

I. **Introduction**
   A. *Who Is the Head of the Church?*
      1. A question that brings conflict
      2. The answer
   B. *Paul Declared Christ to Be the Head of the Church*
   C. *Why Is Christ Called the Head of the Church?*
      1. Why does He merit this position?
      2. How should this affect local churches?

II. **Body**
   A. *Christ Is to Have the Preeminence in the Church (v. 18)*
      1. He is before all things (He is eternal)
      2. He is the living one (the firstborn from the dead)
         a. His resurrection proves His deity (Rom. 1:4)
         b. His resurrection is also the sign of His authority (John 2:18–22)
      3. No earthly office approaches His position
         a. He has given gifts to the church (Eph. 4:11)
         b. These gifted people serve Him in the church
         c. They draw their authority from Him
      4. Local authority must be carried out in love (1 Cor. 13)
      5. Church leaders ought to be Christlike in serving Him
      6. How Christlike are we?
   B. *Christ Has Made Peace for the Church (v. 20)*
      1. Christ made peace for us at the cross
         a. His blood paid for our sins (1 Peter 1:18–19)
         b. He bought the church with His blood
      2. Christ has reconciled us to Himself
         a. This is made personal by faith (Rom. 5:8–9)
         b. This faith brings peace with God (Rom. 5:1)
      3. The reconciliation made at the cross has affected all things
         a. This includes all things on earth and in heaven, both experience and expectation
         b. Nothing on earth or in heaven can separate us from His love (Rom. 8:38–39)

125

C. *Christf Presents the Church Perfect in Heaven
   (vv. 21–22)*
   1. Our perfect Savior presents us perfect
      a. Aliens have been made part of God's family
      b. Enemies have become the recipients of His
         grace
   2. Wicked ones have been reconciled to the Holy One
      a. Sinners are presented unblamable by the head
         of the church
      b. Faulty ones are presented unreproveable
         before the throne
   3. Who can measure such grace or understand such
      love?

III. **Conclusion**
   A. *Does Christ Have First Place in Our Church?*
      1. In our worship and business?
      2. If not, why not?
   B. *Let's Make Christ the Head of Our Church and Our
      Lives*

The Hope of Glory

I. **Introduction**
   A. *Paul, a Mystery Writer*
      1. The mystery of the times of the Gentiles (Rom. 11:25)
      2. The mystery of the age of grace (Rom. 16:25)
      3. The mystery of the coming rapture (1 Cor. 16:51)
   B. *The Greatest Mystery of All*
      1. A mystery hidden from Old Testament saints (1:26)
      2. The mystery of Christ within believers, the hope of glory (1:27)
   C. *The Three Choices of Hope*

II. **Body**
   A. *False Hope (1 Cor. 15:19)*
      1. False hopes ultimately make one miserable
      2. Some people hope in money (Luke 18:23)
         a. The rich young ruler came to Jesus
         b. Many are like him, making money their god
      3. Some people hope in their intellect or abilities
         a. They believe that education answers all needs
         b. They think that they can handle any crisis
      4. Some people hope in religious ceremonies or rites
      5. Some people hope in their good works
      6. Christ is risen so hope in Him is sure
   B. *No Hope (Eph. 2:12)*
      1. To live without Christ is to die without hope
         a. Hope is tested at death
         b. Earthly successes will be no comfort then
      2. Contrasts of hope at death (1 Thess. 4:13)
         a. Believers do not sorrow like the lost
         b. Unbelievers have no sure hope at death
      3. Comfort at death is only for believers
         a. Unbelievers borrow Christian comfort
         b. Eternal promises are only for Christians
      4. There are no promises of hope for those who die in unbelief

   C. *The Hope of Glory (1:27)*
1. "Christ in you, the hope of glory"
2. Not hoping *for* glory
   a. Hope here is a confident expectation
   b. G. Campbell Morgan: "Does not mean foundationless expectation but rather confidence in something."
3. What is the reason for this confidence?
   a. The resurrection brings living hope (1 Peter 1:3)
   b. Glory is ahead for sufferers here (Rom. 8:18)

III. Conclusion
   A. *Invite the Living Christ into Your Life*
   B. *Choose the Hope of Glory*

Walking Safely on the Danger Trail

Series in Colossians   *Colossians 2*

I. **Introduction**
  A. *The Danger Trail*
    1. Paul's concern for the Colossian Christians (v. 1)
    2. A warning about enticements to sin and error (v. 4)
    3. The key word in the chapter: "Beware" (v. 8)
  B. *The Secrets of Safety*
    1. How to walk after being born again
    2. Simple secrets for safety on the journey

II. **Body**
  A. *Walk as You Have Received Christ Jesus the Lord (v. 6)*
    1. It is important to stay close to the conversion experience
      a. How serious sin seemed!
      b. How wonderful God's love seemed!
      c. How sensible faith seemed!
    2. We must remember our first love for Christ (Rev. 2:1–5)
    3. Gypsy Smith: "I have never lost the wonder of it all."
    4. We must walk by faith in the wonder of His love
  B. *Walk Rooted in Christ Jesus the Lord (v. 7)*
    1. "Rooted and built up in him"
    2. We should be like the roots of a tree
      a. Reaching out to take in water (the Holy Spirit)
      b. Absorbing nutrients for growth from the Word
    3. We find all we need in Christ (vv. 8–9)
      a. Not in philosophy but in faith
      b. Not in the world but in the Word
  C. *Walk Refreshed in Christ Jesus the Lord (v. 7)*
    1. "As ye have been taught"
    2. Old truths about Christ keep refreshing us (v. 10)
      a. We are complete in Him
      b. He is more powerful than our enemies
    3. We are made alive; we've been forgiven (vv. 13–15)

        a. The debt of our transgressions of the law has
been paid
        b. Satan and his demons are defeated
  D. *Walk Rejoicing in Christ Jesus the Lord (v. 7)*
      1. "Abounding . . . with thanksgiving"
      2. We are saved by grace and thankful for it
        a. No longer in bondage to the law (vv. 16–18)
        b. Dead to sin and alive in Christ (vv. 19–23)
      3. We rejoice in our victorious Lord

III. Conclusion
  A. *Dangers to Avoid*
      1. Pride, false teachers, and legalism
      2. God's grace is sufficient for our every need
  B. *Walking by Faith, We're Safe on the Danger Trail*

Risen with Christ

Colossians 4:1–4

I. **Introduction**
   A. *"If" Is the Biggest Little Word in the World*
      1. Determines life or death, heaven or hell
      2. Demands that believers walk their talk
   B. *Paul Challenges Us to Look Alive*
      1. "If ye then be risen with Christ"
      2. Advice and encouragement for living ones

II. **Body**
   A. *Two Great Commandments (vv. 1–2)*
      1. "Seek those things which are above"
         a. Learn all you can about heaven, your future home
         b. Search for truth about that blessed place
         c. Seek like a shepherd seeks lost sheep (Luke 19:10)
      2. "Set your affection on things above"
         a. What we love tells who we are (Matt. 6:21)
         b. Most people set their affection on things below
         c. Those who are risen with Christ must love higher things
      3. What are you seeking in life?
      4. What has first place in your heart?
   B. *Two Great Consolations*
      1. "For ye are dead'"
         a. What kind of consolation is this?
         b. What does Paul mean when he says we are all dead?
      2. We are dead to sin and alive to God (Rom. 6:11)
      3. We are crucified with Christ, yet alive in Him (Gal. 2:20)
      4. "Your life is hid with Christ in God"
         a. All the treasures of wisdom are hidden in Christ (Col. 2:3)
         b. We are hidden with these treasures
         c. What a safe place to be!

C. *Two Great Coming Events (v. 4)*
1. Christ shall appear
   a. The promise of Jesus (John 14:1–3)
   b. The promise of angels (Acts 1:10–11)
   c. The promise of Paul (1 Thess. 4:13–18)
2. We shall appear with Him in glory
   a. Believers are coming back with Jesus at the rapture (1 Thess. 4:14)
   b. The blessed hope and glorious appearing (Titus 2:13)
   c. We will receive glorious bodies (Phil. 3:20–21)
   d. We will be with Christ forever (1 Thess. 4:17)
   e. We will be like Jesus (1 John 3:2)

III. Conclusion
A. *The Biggest Little Word in the World Is "If"*
B. *If You Have Received Christ, the Future Is Bright*
C. *If You Reject Him, You Have No Hope*

Getting Dressed for the Day

Series in Colossians   *Colossians 3:8–14*

I. **Introduction**
  A. *Great Doctrines Make Great Daily Living*
    1. It's not enough merely to agree to certain doctrines
    2. We must translate our beliefs into life
  B. *The Colossians Accepted Some Great Doctrines*
    1. Redemption through Christ's blood (1:14)
    2. The preeminence of Christ (1:18)
    3. The indwelling presence of Christ (1:28)
  C. *Paul Calls for These Beliefs to Change Us Every Day*

II. **Body**
  A. *Put Off These Attitudes (vv. 8–9)*
    1. Anger and wrath are destructive to those we love
    2. Malice harbors old grudges and dwells on them
    3. Blasphemy grieves the Holy Spirit
    4. Filthy communication stains our public testimony
    5. Lies make us unlike our Lord, who is the truth
    6. These are all attitudes of darkness
      a. They should be discarded each morning
      b. We are to be lights in a dark world
      c. Why start the day dressed for night?
      d. Let's start each morning dressed for the day
  B. *Put on These Association Builders (vv. 10–13)*
    1. The new man, who grows in the image of Christ
    2. Holiness, which mirrors the integrity of God
    3. Mercy and kindness, which demonstrate grace
    4. Humility, which makes us Christlike
    5. Meekness, which overcomes pride and arrogance
    6. Patience, which shows consideration for others
    7. Forbearance and forgiveness, which break down barriers
    8. All qualities that enable us to bring others to Christ
  C. *Put on Christian Affection, the Mark of Maturity*
    1. "Above all these things put on charity"
    2. Love is the bond that holds everything together (1 Cor. 13)

133

        a. Love reveals a close walk with our loving Lord
        b. Love holds families together in tough times
        c. Love holds churches together and makes
            outreach possible
    3. Love produces unity among believers
    4. Every word and action must be clothed in love
    5. If we love things above, we'll love people here
        below

III. **Conclusion**
    A. *What Do You Need to Put Off?*
    B. *Are You Willing to Put on These Christlike Qualities
        Daily?*
        1. Think what this would do for our church
        2. Think of the impact this would have on our
            community

Those Thankful Colossians

Series in Colossians Ends   *Colossians 3:15, 17; 4:1–2*

I. Introduction
   A. *Thanksgiving in the Heart and Home*
      1. An attitude of gratitude changes everything
      2. It is a powerful influence in all areas of life
   B. *Paul's Goal: To Develop Thankful People*
      1. He knows that thankful hearts will make loving homes and churches
      2. He shows how right it is for believers to be thankful

II. Body
   A. *When the Heart Is Right, Thanksgiving Is Natural (3:14–16)*
      1. "Above all these put on love"
         a. Loving God makes us thankful for His grace
         b. Loving people makes us thankful for family and friends
      2. The peace of God comes to a thankful heart (Phil. 4:6–8)
      3. See what a thankful heart brings to us (v. 16)
         a. We're prepared to receive the word of Christ
         b. Wisdom results from receiving His Word
         c. We teach and are taught from the Scriptures
         d. The joy of thanksgiving fills us with song
      4. How can we get our hearts right so that we will be thankful people?
         a. We must confess our sins so that we are right with God (1 John 1:9)
         b. We must forgive those who have wronged us so that we are right with others
   B. *When the Life Is Right, Thanksgiving Is Normal (3:17–4:1)*
      1. Paul's formula for normal Christian living
         a. We do everything in the name of Jesus
         b. We give thanks for everything
      2. How living thankfully affects family living
         a. Thankful husbands love their wives deeply

   b. Thankful wives build up their loving husbands

   c. Thankful children obey their parents

   d. Thankful parents are considerate of their children

  3. Thanksgiving in the workplace

   a. Thankful workers give superior service in gratitude to God

   b. Thankful employers treat workers as God treats them

 C. *When Prayers Are Right, Thanksgiving Is Never Neglected (4:2)*

  1. "Continue in prayer"

   a. Pray when life is good and when trouble comes

   b. Keep on praying even when answers seem slow in coming

  2. "Watch in the same with thanksgiving"

   a. Expect God to answer in His time

   b. Give thanks for answers to prayer before they arrive

III. **Conclusion**

 A. *What Has This Powerful Epistle Taught Us?*

 B. *How Can We Apply These Important Teachings to Our Lives?*

 C. *How Many Will Give Christ the Preeminence Starting Today?*

Church Homecoming

Ecclesiastes 3:1

I. Introduction

A. *It's Time to Come Home*
  1. Many people have responded to this homecoming call
  2. Some of you have traveled long distances to come home

B. *What's Homecoming All About?*
  1. Why are we here?
  2. What will this homecoming accomplish?

II. Body

A. *Homecoming Is a Time to Remember*
  1. A time to remember faithful people
     a. Those who started the church long ago
     b. Those who kept praying and serving in tough times
     c. Those who taught and brought others to Christ
  2. A time to remember faithful pastors
  3. A time to remember great steps of faith
     a. Those who dared to move ahead when funds were low and debts were high
     b. Those who had courage to build when timid ones trembled at the challenge
  4. A time to remember examples of Christian love
     a. Caring for the sick in the membership
     b. Coming to the aid of those in trouble
  5. A time to remember when people came to Christ and all rejoiced

B. *Homecoming Is a Time to Forget*
  1. Paul wrote about a time to forget (Phil. 3:13)
  2. What shall we forget?
     a. Forget old wounds that keep feeding malice
     b. Forget the failures of those who have let us down
     c. Forget the sins of those who stumbled along the journey
     d. Forget our own failures that still bring discouragement

137

      3. Refusing to forget old wrongs stops forward progress

          a. God has forgiven us so we should forgive others (Eph. 4:31–32)

          b. Unless we let go, we cannot grow

   C. *Homecoming Is a Time to Recapture Vision*

      1. What was the vision of those who started the church?

      2. What is the state of that vision today?

          a. Has the original vision been lost?

          b. Do we expect as much for the church now as they did then?

      3. Without a vision, the people perish (Prov. 29:18)

      4. How much do we dare to trust God to do here in the future?

      5. Can we believe that God will do greater things than He did in the past?

III. **Conclusion**

   A. *Let's Return to Our First Love of Christ (Rev. 2:4–5)*

   B. *Let's Love Souls as Our Lord Loves Them*

   C. *Let's Labor in His Harvest, Expecting Much Fruit*

   D. *Let's Make This Church More Effective Than Ever Before*

Who Is Jesus?

Acts 9:5

I. **Introduction**
   A. *Saul's Searching Question*
      1. Saul was passionate in persecuting the church
      2. Jesus confronted Saul on the road to Damascus
         a. A light from heaven; a voice speaking to him
         b. Saul's question: "Who art thou, Lord?"
         c. The voice's answer: "I am Jesus. . . ."
   B. *But Who Is Jesus?*

II. **Body**
   A. *He Is the Prophesied Savior*
      1. The first promise of a Savior came after the fall (Gen. 3:15)
         a. The One to bruise the serpent's head
         b. The One to redeem a sinful race
      2. The prophets added their voices
         a. The Savior to be virgin born (Isa. 7:14)
         b. The Savior to be God in flesh (Isa. 7:14; 9:6–7)
         c. The Savior to be born in Bethlehem (Mic. 5:2)
         d. The Savior to be preceded by John, who would prepare the way (Isa. 40:3)
      3. The miraculous birth occurred in Bethlehem (Luke 2)
         a. The Roman Empire was a part of the miracle (the taxing)
         b. Christ was born right on time (Gal. 4:4–5)
   B. *He Is the Crucified Savior*
      1. Every step Jesus took in life was toward the cross
         a. Isaiah had prophesied His painful death for sinners (Isa. 53)
         b. John the Baptist called Him the Lamb of God (John 1:36)
      2. Jesus revealed his coming death to His disciples (Matt. 20:18–19)
      3. On the cross, He was the figure of forgiveness (Matt. 27:29–50)

            a.   Even the dying thief found forgiveness (Luke 23:43)

            b.   All who come to Him find forgiveness and eternal life (John 3:16; 6:37)

C. *He Is the Risen Savior*

    1.   His resurrection proved His deity (John 2:19)

    2.   His enemies thought that they had destroyed Him at the cross

            a.   But He arose (Matt. 28:1–6)

            b.   Because He arose, those who trust Him will also rise (1 Cor. 15:20)

    3.   Many proofs of His resurrection

            a.   The empty tomb and the eyewitnesses

            b.   The transformed disciples and the enduring church

D. *He Is the Coming Savior*

    1.   Christ, who died and rose again, will come again

    2.   He must come to fulfill His promise (John 14:1–3)

    3.   Are you ready for His return?

III. Conclusion

A. *Saul Found Out Who Jesus Was by Trusting Him as Savior*

B. *Faith in Jesus Will Answer Your Questions About Him, Too*

A Stroll Through the First Cemetery

Genesis 5:6–24

I. **Introduction**
   A. *Interesting Old Cemeteries*
      1. Epitaphs tell the history of a community
         a. They often illustrate the depth of Christian faith
         b. They sometimes reveal the visitations of past plagues
         c. They might bring tears to tenderhearted people who notice the number of early deaths
      2. They all demonstrate that death is an appointment we all keep (Heb. 9:27)
   B. *Truths from a Text About Life and Death*

II. **Body**
   A. *Death Is Very Certain (vv. 5–14)*
      1. Death had been promised for taking of the forbidden fruit (2:3)
         a. Satan cast doubt on this in the first temptation (2:4)
         b. Death entered with the first sin and has reigned ever since (Rom. 5:12–14)
      2. Abel was the first person to die at the hand of another (Gen. 4:8)
      3. Adam was the first person to die a natural death—at 930 years (v. 5)
      4. The length of life recorded on these biblical tombstones is revealing
         a. We do not know why such longevity was the rule
         b. God still determines the life span of us all
         c. Death may be long in coming for some, but it will arrive for all
      5. Death's sure march calls for preparation for eternity
      6. No one is prepared to live until he is prepared to die

141

    B. *Life Is Very Uncertain (vv. 15–20)*
1. Note the different ages at death
   a. Do you think of death as only for the old?
   b. "Remember now thy creator in the days of thy youth" (Eccl. 12:1)
   c. The first person to die was a young man (Abel); violence takes many of the young
2. Life is as uncertain as the withering of grass (1 Peter 1:24)
3. Life is as uncertain as a vapor that appears and vanishes (James 4:14)
4. The old must die, and the young may die
5. Remember the rich fool who expected to live for many years
   a. He thought that he could retire and take it easy
   b. He died the day of his boast of a lifetime of plenty (Luke 12:20)

    C. *Let Us Walk with God and Live Forever (vv. 21–24)*
1. Enoch was a man who walked with God
   a. He is a beacon of light in a dark chapter
   b. He is an example of life in a chapter of death
2. We walk with God by faith (Rom. 5:1; 2 Cor. 5:7)
3. Faith brings salvation and eternal life (Eph. 2:8–9)
4. Enoch pictures believers who will be raptured when Christ returns

III. Conclusion
    A. *Will You Receive Christ by Faith Today?*
    B. *He Alone Offers Eternal Life*
1. Eternal life begins the moment you believe (1 John 5:12)
2. You can know that you will live forever (1 John 5:13)

The Last Enemy

1 Corinthians 15:26

I. Introduction

A. *Man Was Created to Live*
1. Man became a living soul (Gen. 2:7)
2. He was created for unbroken fellowship with God

B. *Death Came Because of Sin*
1. This was the one restriction in a perfect place (Gen. 3:3)
2. Disobedience brought death (Rom. 5:12–14)

II. Body

A. *Death Is an Enemy That Stalks Us All*
1. "It is appointed unto man once to die" (Heb. 9:27)
   a. This is an appointment that we all must keep
   b. Other appointments can be canceled, but not this one
2. This enemy may overtake us in many ways
   a. Sometimes in youth, even infancy
   b. Sometimes in old age—our bodies wear out
   c. Sometimes through fatal accidents
3. Some people lose the battle for life by cooperating with the enemy
   a. Accidents caused by alcohol and other drugs
   b. Smoking and other habits that hasten death
4. Many deaths are the result of domestic violence and crime
5. The enemy claims many lives through war

B. *Death Is an Enemy Our Savior Has Engaged*
1. Christ came to taste death for each of us (Heb. 2:9)
   a. He voluntarily became lower than the angels
   b. He humbled Himself, even to death (Phil. 2:5–7)
2. The enemy pursued Him from Bethlehem to Calvary
   a. Herod's slaughter of the children of Bethlehem (Matt. 2:16–18)
   b. The attempt to cast Christ down from a hill (Luke 4:29)

      c. The attempt to kill Christ by stoning (John 10:31)

      d. Satan's temptation to get Jesus to commit suicide (Matt. 4:6)

      e. Jesus' near-death experience in Gethsemane (Matt. 26:36)

   3. Christ had come to engage death on the cross

      a. He voluntarily laid down His life (John 10:17)

      b. He was in full control to the end (Luke 23:46)

C. *Death Is an Enemy That Christ Defeated*

   1. Death has been defeated by the resurrection (1 Cor. 15:20)

      a. His resurrection demonstrated His victory

      b. His resurrection guarantees our resurrection

   2. Death is defeated by the promise of heaven (John 14:1–3)

   3. Death is defeated by the promise of the coming rapture (1 Thess. 3:13–18)

III. Conclusion

A. *Death Will Finally Be Destroyed*

B. *Death Will Be No More (Rev. 21:4)*

C. *Are You Ready for That Great Day?*

Joseph in Jeopardy

Genesis 39

I. Introduction
   A. *Joseph: A Man Who Came Through Trials Triumphantly*
      1. His brothers hated him and sold him into slavery for twenty pieces of silver
      2. He was imprisoned and mistreated although he was innocent of all charges
      3. He provided food to multitudes in a time of famine
   B. *Joseph: A Reminder of Jesus*
      1. Jesus was rejected by His own (John 1:10–12)
      2. Jesus was sold for thirty pieces of silver (Matt. 26:15)
      3. Jesus was faithful when tempted and has blessed multitudes (Matt. 4)
   C. *Joseph: His Testimony, Temptation, and Triumph*

II. Body
   A. *The Testimony of Joseph (vv. 1–6)*
      1. His master, Potiphar, saw that the Lord was with him
         a. There was something different about Joseph
         b. The only answer was that God was with him
         c. Do others see this difference in us?
      2. Joseph had a servant's heart: "he served"
         a. Joseph was a worker as we are to be (Col. 3:23)
         b. Joseph's work was consistent with his walk
      3. Joseph's faithful service led to greater opportunities
      4. Joseph was blessed and became a blessing (vv. 5–6)
   B. *The Temptation of Joseph (vv. 7–12)*
      1. Joseph's master's wife tempted him
      2. Temptation comes to all of us
         a. It is not sinful to be tempted
         c. It is sin to yield to temptation
      3. Temptation can come from unexpected sources
      4. Temptation can be persistent in its attacks on us

        a. Potiphar's wife kept after Joseph "day by day"

        b. We must stay diligent at all times

  5. We ought to avoid situations that increase temptation (vv. 11–12)

        a. Joseph should not have been alone with this temptress

        b. We are to abstain from all appearance of evil (1 Thess. 5:22)

  C. *The Triumph of Joseph (vv. 12–23)*

    1. Joseph was stripped of his clothes but not of his character

        a. Steadfast integrity was more important to Joseph than sexual intrigue

        b. Sometimes the best way to overcome temptation is to flee (1 Cor. 6:18; 10:14)

    2. God provides grace and a way of escape with every temptation (1 Cor. 10:13)

    3. Had Joseph yielded to temptation, he would have remained a slave

    4. Joseph's integrity brought him to jail, but then it exalted him

III. Conclusion

  A. *The Lord Was with Joseph Every Step of the Way (v. 21)*

  B. *This Servant of God Prospered Even in Prison (v. 23)*

  C. *Will We Be Faithful Whatever the Cost?*

The Call of Elisha:
A Man with a Passion for Power

1 Kings 19:19–21

I. **Introduction**
   A. *Elijah at the End of the Trail*
   1. A mighty prophet of God neared the close of his ministry
      a. He challenged wicked King Ahab
      b. He prayed with such power that he stopped the rain for six months
      c. He became the second man in space—after Enoch
      d. He was so important that he met Moses and Jesus at the Transfiguration
   2. Elijah was commissioned to choose Elisha as his successor (v. 17)
   B. *Elisha as a Successful Farmer*
   1. He was plowing with twelve yoke of oxen when Elijah arrived
   2. He was evidently successful and loved doing things in a big way
   3. Now his life would be turned around, and he would never be the same

II. **Body**
   A. *Elisha's Call from the Lord (v. 19)*
   1. The Lord knew Elisha before Elijah arrived (v. 16; 1 Peter 1:2)
   2. The Lord called Elisha before Elijah announced it (Eph. 1:4)
   3. The Lord used Elijah to tell Elisha of His call
      a. God uses His servants to fulfill His will
      b. We should be open to the ministry of the servants of God
   4. The Lord called Elisha to service when he was busy
   5. God's call often demands that we leave worldly success behind to serve Him

147

B. *Elisha's Conflict as He Considered God's Call (v. 20)*
1. The call of God always creates a conflict in our lives
   a. God's call demands a decision to follow Him
   b. Moses must leave his sheep; Peter must leave his boats and fishing
2. Elisha's many problems as he considered God's call
   a. The problem of his parents (loved ones are often involved in a decision)
   b. The problem of his position (who will tend the farm?)
   c. The problem of his passion for power (he loved that field full of hired hands)
3. The battle that many people lose
   a. The rich young ruler lost this battle (Luke 18:18–23)
   b. Will you choose worldly things and lose God's best for your life?

C. *Elisha's Consecration That Emerged from His Conflict (v. 21)*
1. Elisha decided that God would be first in his life
   a. God's call was more important than position or power
   b. Elisha's surrender would give him the position of a prophet of God
   c. Elisha would ultimately be even more powerful than Elijah
2. Elisha made his commitment public
   a. He burned his plow in the field and had a barbecue for his workmen
   b. The neighborhood would know that there was a new prophet on the block

III. Conclusion
A. *How Will You Respond to God's Call on Your Life?*
B. *Will You Count All Things as Loss for Christ?*
C. *Will You Publicly Declare Your Surrender to Him?*

Rewards for Runners

1 Corinthians 9:24–27

I. **Introduction**
  A. *Heavenly Rewards: A Neglected Subject*
    1. We speak more of homes here than in heaven
    2. We talk of security, nest eggs, and promotions but little of eternal rewards
    3. Jesus taught us to lay up treasures in heaven (Matt. 6:19–20)
  B. *Crowns in the Bible*
    1. Special rewards go to those who run life's race well
    2. What's involved in this race, and what are its rewards?

II. **Body**
  A. *The Participants in the Race (v. 24)*
    1. Those who enter this race must begin at the starting point
      a. The starting point in this race is salvation (Acts 16:31; Rom. 10:9)
      b. Not everyone is in the race for heavenly rewards
    2. The unsaved race to hell and keep storing up wrath
      a. Fire awaits at the finish line, and the only prize is perdition
      b. Everything about the sinner's race is temporary, except eternal punishment
    3. Those who have been born again are in life's most important race
      a. Rewards await every believer at the finish line
      b. The finish line is at the judgment seat of Christ
    4. Other texts also speak of this race (Phil. 3:14; Heb. 12:1; 2 Tim. 4:7)
    5. How are you doing in the race?
  B. *The Prize at the End of the Race (vv. 24–25)*
    1. Runners have a prize in view when the race begins
      a. The starter sees himself breaking the tape at the finish line

149

   b.   The prize will keep him pressing on to the end
        of the race
2.   Paul referred to earthly games and corruptible
     crowns of no lasting value
     a.   He probably had in mind the Isthmian games
          at the Corinthian citadel
     b.   The prizes there were garlands of pine (some
          then of parsley, olive, or ivy)
3.   How temporary are the prizes that most people
     seek throughout life!
     a.   Accumulated wealth has no value at life's end
          (1 Tim. 6:7)
     b.   Prestige and popularity are fading rewards that
          often are lost before the finish
4.   Christians race for lasting rewards at Christ's
     return (Rev. 22:12)
C.   *The Price of Running to Win the Prize in This Race
     (vv. 26–27)*
     1.   "I therefore run, not as uncertainly"
          a.   There was no doubt about Paul's intention to
               win the prize
          b.   He didn't have time or energy to waste—
               neither do we
     2.   Paul had his eye fixed on the prize at the finish line
          (Phil. 3:13–14)
     3.   Winning the prize demands strenuous discipline
          and self-denial
          a.   Paul brought his body into subjection, not
               giving in to lust or laziness
          b.   We ought to be willing to pay the price of this
               winner's example

III.   **Conclusion**
       A.   *Enter the Race to Eternal Rewards by Faith in Christ*
       B.   *Gain Eternal Rewards by Surrendering All to Him*

Building Dedication

2 Chronicles 5:1, 13–14; 7:1, 14

I. **Introduction**
   A. *We Have Been Building for the Lord (v. 1)*
      1. We have responded to a God-given vision
      2. We have given money to bring this vision to reality
      3. We have given of our time and talents
   B. *This Is God's Plan for Our Time*
      1. Local churches are God's instruments of outreach
      2. Churches need buildings in which to meet for worship
   C. *What Are the Purposes to Which We Dedicate This Building?*

II. **Body**
   A. *A Place of Rich Praise (vv. 13–14)*
      1. Thanksgiving and praise are vital to worship
         a. See how this was true in the dedication of Solomon's temple
         b. Consider the use of thanksgiving and praise in Psalms
      2. The music makers were busy in dedicating the temple
         a. The choir and the orchestra became as one in praise
         b. Let us raise our voices in thanksgiving and praise in this place
      3. Thanksgiving and praise are valuable
         a. Thanksgiving and praise turn our hearts from conflict to Christ
         b. Thanksgiving and praise lift us from depression to delight
      4. Let thanksgiving and praise fill this building as long as it stands
   B. *A Place of Real Prayer (7:1)*
      1. Solomon prayed, and the fire of God came down to the temple
      2. We need the fire of God to ignite and warm this place

151

      a. This is a troubled time for the world
      b. It is time to bring our problems to the Lord
  3. D. L. Moody states, "Every great work of God can be traced to a kneeling figure."
  4. Backsliding begins in the knees
  5. Churches seem so powerless today
      a. Our well-oiled machinery isn't up to the occasion
      b. Only earnest church-wide prayer can meet the needs of the hour
      c. We need less entertainment and more intercession

C. *A Place of Revival Power (7:14)*
  1. Solomon's dedication was a day of victory, but trials lay ahead
      a. Locusts would visit the land
      b. Pestilence would come among the people
  2. The Lord gave Solomon a promise for the tough times
      a. The people were to pray and seek His face
      b. The people were to turn from their wicked ways
      c. The people would experience revival and healing
  3. Let this building ever be a place of revival and evangelism

III. Conclusion
  A. *Let Us Dedicate This Building by Dedicating Ourselves*
  B. *God Will Meet Us Here and Heal Our Church and Land*

Treasures, Trials, and Testings

1 Peter 1:1–9

I. **Introduction**
   A. *Christians Are Different*
      1. Once they were lost, but now they are found
      2. Once they were bound for hell, but now they are bound for heaven
      3. They are citizens of heaven traveling through this world (Phil. 3:20)
   B. *What Makes Christians React Differently?*
      1. They have found a new reason for living
      2. They have discovered answers that set them apart
   C. *Why Do Christians Have a Different View of Live?*

II. **Body**
   A. *Their Treasures Are Eternal (vv. 1–5)*
      1. They know that nothing takes God by surprise
         a. They are elect according to the foreknowledge of God
         b. They have been in God's plan from the beginning
      2. They know that they have been set apart by the Holy Spirit
         a. They have been cleansed by the blood of Christ
         b. They are recipients of the grace of God
         c. They have found peace
      3. The resurrection of Christ provides them a living hope
      4. They have an eternal inheritance awaiting in heaven
      5. They are kept by God's power and will be with Him forever
   B. *Their Troubles Are Temporary (v. 6)*
      1. They have many causes to rejoice
         a. Their sins are forgiven
         b. They have eternal life
      2. They are not immune to trouble, but they know it will not last

153

        a. Their position in Christ is permanent
        b. Discouragement is only "for a season"
    3. This was Paul's reason for rejoicing in trouble
        a. He could praise in prison and give thanks in persecution
        b. Consider his dungeon doxology in the Philippian jail (Acts 16:25–32)
    4. Finally God will wipe away all tears from their eyes (Rev. 21:4)

C. *Their Trials Are Filled with the Purposes of God (vv. 7–9)*
    1. All believers live in the circle of God's love
        a. Nothing comes their way without His knowledge
        b. All things work together for their good (Rom. 8:28)
        c. Every experience is designed to make them like Jesus (Rom. 8:29)
    2. Trials test their faith to prove that it's real
        a. Like Job, the believer comes out of the fire like gold (Job 23:10)
        b. Temporary trials will result in triumphant eternal praise
    3. Life's present passing problems will seem small when we see Christ

III. Conclusion
    A. *Troubled Sinners Can Come to Christ and Receive Eternal Life*
    B. *Troubled Believers Can Find Comfort in the Promises of God*

Will You Receive Christ or Reject Him?

John 1:10–14

I. Introduction

    A. Beginnings by Gospel Writers

        1. Matthew begins with Abraham, presenting Christ as the king of the Jews

        2. Mark begins with John the Baptist, presenting Christ as the lowly servant

        3. Luke begins with the manger, presenting Christ as the Son of man

        4. John begins at the beginning, presenting Christ as the Son of God

    B. How Did the World React to the Coming of the Son of God?

II. Body

    A. The Rejection of the Word by the World (v. 10)

        1. "He was in the world . . . and the world knew him not"

        2. Christ was presented as the Creator

            a. "All things were made by him" (v. 3)

            b. "The world was made by him" (v. 10)

        3. Proof was offered that Christ was the Creator during his earthly ministry

            a. Turning the water into wine (John 2:1–11)

            b. Walking on the water (John 6:19–20)

            c. Raising the dead (John 11:43–44)

        4. Still, the world rejected Him

            a. Herod was too busy with lust and greed to accept Him

            b. Pilate was too busy playing politics to accept Him

            c. The rich young ruler was too busy making money to accept Him

    B. The Rejection of Jesus by the Jews (v. 11)

        1. "He came unto his own and his own received him not"

        2. The Jews had been waiting for the Messiah, yet they did not recognize Him

       a. The Hebrew prophets had announced that He would come

       b. They gave specific instructions about His birth, death, and resurrection

    3. Christ fulfilled the requirements of the prophets

       a. He was born of a virgin in Bethlehem (Isa. 7:14; Mic. 5:2)

       b. He was wounded and died for sinners (Isa. 53; Zech. 12:10; 13:6)

       c. He arose from the grave (Ps. 16:10)

    4. Still His own people did not receive Him

C. *The Rebirth of Those Who Receive Jesus as Savior (v. 12–13)*

    1. "As many as received him"

       a. Jews or Gentiles can receive Him

       b. Whosoever will may come (John 3:16; 6:37)

    2. Those who receive Christ by faith are born again

       a. Nicodemas learned this when he came to Jesus by night (John 3:1–5)

       b. Those who receive Christ are born into God's family (v. 13)

    3. Have you been born again?

III. Conclusion

A. *The One Who Was Before All Flesh Became Flesh (v. 14)*

B. *The One Who Was in Heaven Came to Earth (Phil. 2:5–7)*

    1. He came to earth that we might go to heaven (John 14:1–6)

    2. Will you receive Christ or reject Him?

Paul Before Felix

Acts 24:1–23

I. **Introduction**
  A. *Paul Was Determined to Go to Jerusalem*
    1. The Holy Spirit had warned him of bonds and afflictions there (Acts 20:23)
    2. Disciples, speaking by the Holy Spirit, told him not to go (21:4)
    3. Many other believers begged him not to go (21:12)
  B. *Paul Had Trouble in Jerusalem (Acts 22–23)*
    1. Telling of his conversion brought persecution and arrest
    2. Appealing his rights as a Roman citizen sent to Caesarea
  C. *Paul Appeared Before Felix, the Roman Governor*

II. **Body**
  A. *Paul's Accusers (24:1–9)*
    1. Tertullus, an eloquent lawyer, began by praising Felix (vv. 2–3)
    2. He presented three false charges against Paul
      a. He was pestilent, a disturber of the peace (v. 5)
      b. He was a mover of sedition among all Jews (v. 5)
      c. He was a profaner of the temple (v. 6)
    3. Believers can expect to be accused falsely
      a. Jesus was accused falsely, so we must expect the same treatment
      b. A servant is not greater than his Lord (John 15:20)
    4. One charge against Paul was true: he was a leader among Christians (v. 5)
    5. The world rejects and persecutes those who love Christ and serve Him (2 Tim. 3:12)
  B. *Paul Answered His Accusers (vv. 10–15)*
    1. He answered cheerfully (v. 10)
      a. Some people might have given in to discouragement
      b. Some people would have been bitter toward their accusers

157

      2. He answered truthfully (vv. 11–13)
        a. He had not gone to Jerusalem to cause a riot
        b. He had gone to Jerusalem to worship God
      3. He confessed that he was a believer in Christ
        (vv. 14–15)
        a. He insisted that he worshiped according to the
          words of the prophets
        b. He admitted that he believed in a resurrection
          of the just and the unjust
      4. Paul's truthful answers made his accusers
        accountable to God
   C. *Paul Shared His Aim in Life with Felix (vv. 16–21)*
      1. Paul wanted to have a conscience void of offense
        toward God and men
        a. Paul wanted to be continually right with God
        b. He also wanted to be right with people
        c. How do your aims compare with those of
          Paul?
      2. Paul wanted to be generous, bringing gifts to the
        poor of his people
      3. Paul wanted Felix to know that the resurrection is
        important (Rom. 10:9)
      4. Are you right with both God and people?
      5. Are you ready for Christ's return and the
        resurrection?

III. Conclusion
   A. *Felix Now Understood More About the Gospel*
      (vv. 22–23)
   B. *Do Others Know More About the Gospel Because of*
      You?

Felix Before Paul

Acts 24:24–27

I. Introduction

A. *Things Are Seldom What They Seem*
1. We see events and experiences from an earthly point of view
2. God sees everything from a heavenly point of view
3. The Holy Spirit enables believers to get in on the heavenly view (1 Cor. 2:14–16)

B. *Paul Stood Before Felix, but Felix Was Really Before Paul*
1. Paul would share heaven's message with this earthly judge
2. The response of the judge would determine his eternal destiny

II. Body

A. *Felix the Man (v. 24)*
1. Antonius Felix was the governor of Judea
   a. Appointed to this position by Claudius Caesar
   b. Appointed to this position about two years before meeting Paul
2. There are not many good things to say about Felix
   a. He was an unprincipled, ungodly, scheming politician
   b. He had his own version of "Murder, Inc.," to eliminate his enemies
3. What about Drusilla?
   a. She was the youngest and most beautiful daughter of King Agrippa I
   b. She had married King Azizus but was lured from him by Felix
4. Paul, the prisoner, found himself standing before two guilty people
5. When Paul spoke, he had a message to change the governor's life

B. *Felix and Paul's Message to Him (v. 25)*
1. Paul's three-point outline was straight from God to the governor

    2. Point one: righteousness
      a. We are all without it (Rom. 3:23)
      b. Our man-made righteousness is as filthy rags (Isa. 64:6)
      c. Our only hope of righteousness is through faith (Rom. 4:3)
    3. Point two: temperance (self-control)
      a. This word is used only three times in the Bible: here, Galatians 5:23; and 2 Peter 1:6
      b. Felix was a controller out of control; he was interested in controlling others
      c. Christ offers self-control to those who can't control their lusts and habits
    4. Point three: judgment to come
      a. What courage this demanded of Paul!
      b. He told the judge that he would someday be judged
      c. We all need to face this truth and prepare for its fulfillment (Heb. 9:27)
  C. *Felix and His Mistake (v. 25)*
    1. Felix trembled as Paul finished his message
      a. God was at work in his heart, convicting him of sin
      b. This was the moment of opportunity for the governor
    2. Felix chose to procrastinate
    3. It is always a mistake to put off turning to Christ

III. Conclusion
  A. *Has God Been Speaking to You About Getting Right with Him?*
  B. *There Will Never Be a More Convenient Time to Be Saved*

How to Become a New Person

2 Corinthians 5:17–19

I. **Introduction**
   A. *Nutshell Bible Verses*
      1. The gospel in a nutshell (John 3:16)
      2. The Christian life in a nutshell (2 Cor. 5:17)
   B. *When One Comes to Christ, All Things Become New*
      1. This is not strange since trusting Christ brings new birth (John 3:1–5)
      2. Jesus told religious Nicodemus that he needed to be born again
      3. Being born again results in a new life
   C. *A Description of What Happens After Conversion*

II. **Body**
   A. *The Fading Things (v. 17)*
      1. "Old things are passed away"
      2. Paul wrote from personal experience
         a. Once he had hoped to destroy the church
         b. Now he gave his life to starting and building up churches
      3. Bible examples of old things passing away
         a. "Ye were the servants of sin" (Rom. 6:17)
         b. "And such were some of you" (1 Cor. 6:9–11)
         c. "You hath he quickened, who were dead in trespasses and sins" (Eph. 2:1–3)
      4. The Christian life is a changed life, and this change is evident to all
      5. Something is wrong if nothing changes when you say you're born again
   B. *The Fresh Things (v. 17)*
      1. "Behold, all things are become new"
      2. The departure of old things does not signal a vacuum but a victory
      3. Trusting in Christ gives a new start; sins are forgiven (1 Cor. 6:11)
      4. Being born again brings a new purpose for living (Phil. 3:7–10)

    5. Receiving Jesus as Savior means the believer has a new destination—heaven

    6. Becoming a Christian provides a new outlook on life

        a. Not how much we can get, but how much we can give

        b. Not how many at the bar, but how many at the altar

        c. Not how much prestige, but how much power in prayer

        d. Not a life based on lust, but a life based on love for believers and the lost

  C. *The Foundation of All Things (v. 18)*

    1. "All things are of God"

    2. All things work together for our good, fulfilling God's purposes (Rom. 8:28)

    3. We have nothing to boast about, for all that we receive or achieve is from the Lord

    4. We have nothing to fret about, for He cares for us and holds our future in His hands

    5. We have no need to get revenge for wrongs, for God ultimately makes everything right

III. Conclusion

  A. *Faith in Christ Reconciles Us to God (v. 18)*

    1. This is the greatest love story ever told

    2. Guilty sinners are reconciled to God, and He gives them new life

  B. *New People Want Others to Be Made New (v. 19)*

  C. *One Headed for Heaven Will Want Others to Go There, Too*

The Unsearchable Riches of Christ

Ephesians 3:8

I. **Introduction**
   A. *The World Searches Madly for Riches*
      1. People will sacrifice almost anything for wealth
      2. Heaven itself has been sold for a pittance in gold
      3. Judas sold Jesus for thirty pieces of silver
   B. *The Riches of This World Are Temporary*
      1. "Lay not up for yourselves treasures on earth" (Matt. 6:19)
      2. "Riches profit not in the day of wrath" (Prov. 11:4)
   C. *Paul Preferred the Unsearchable Riches of Christ*

II. **Body**
   A. *The Riches of His Goodness (Rom. 2:4)*
      1. How good the Lord has been to us!
         a. He has given us life with all of its blessings
         b. He has provided eternal life through His death on the cross
      2. His goodness is manifested in His forbearance (patience)
         a. He holds back the judgment we deserve
         b. He puts up with our many failures and sins
      3. His long-suffering demonstrates His wonderful love
      4. Understanding His goodness leads us to repentance
         a. How can we resist such love?
         b. He reaches out to us where we are, to make us what we ought to be
   B. *The Riches of His Grace (Eph. 2:7)*
      1. Grace: what a wonderful and all-encompassing word!
         a. A word that combines the love and mercy of God
         b. A word that invites sinners to the Savior to be cleansed and made whole
      2. Grace rescues and revives those who are dead in sin (Eph. 2:1–3)

163

   3. There is nothing good about these sinners who are
      offered grace
      a. They had been walking according to the course
         of this world
      b. They had been fulfilling the lusts of the flesh
         (5:1–6)
   4. The future is bright for those who receive the
      riches of His grace
      a. They are secure for the future (the ages to
         come)
      b. They will forever be the objects of His
         kindness
C. *The Riches of His Glory (Eph. 1:18)*
   1. This has to do with our inheritance with Christ
      a. We are heirs of God and joint heirs with Christ
         (Rom. 8:17)
      b. We will receive this rich inheritance when our
         Lord returns (Rom. 8:18)
   2. Now believers look at creation and glory
   3. Then creation will look at believers and glory
   4. Peter, James, and John caught a glimpse of His
      glory on the Mount of Transfiguration (Matt. 16)
   5. We will share the riches of His glory throughout
      eternity

III. Conclusion
   A. *What Poor Sinner Will Accept Rich Grace Today?*
   B. *Who Will Believe That Our Savior Is Rich Enough in
      Mercy to Save?*
   C. *Who Longs to Share in the Riches of God's Glory
      Forever?*

Break Up Your Fallow Ground

Hosea 10:12

I. **Introduction**
A. *The Gospel and the Great Commission*
1. The gospel makes salvation available to all (Rom. 10:9–13)
2. The Great Commission sends believers with the gospel to all (Matt. 28:18–20)
3. The gospel preached by the early church turned the world upside down (Acts 17:6)
B. *We Need to Return to Those Thrilling Days of Yesteryear*
1. We need a revival that restores first love and a passion for the lost
2. We need a revival just as they needed it in Hosea's day
a. The people needed to break up their fallow ground
b. What did Hosea mean when he called for this to happen among his people?

II. **Body**
A. *What Is Fallow Ground?*
1. Fallow ground was once productive but now lies waste
a. Once there were abundant harvests from this soil
b. Now there are but weeds and wilderness
2. Hosea could identify with the need to break up the fallow ground
a. Israel's glorious past: the Red Sea miracle, manna, and water from a rock
b. The nation's sad condition that prompted Hosea's prophetic call
3. We can identify with the need for this call in our time
a. Churches have grown cold and compromising
b. Saints sit and soak while sinners die and go to hell

    B. *What Does Fallow Ground Produce?*
       1. Fallow ground produces thorns and thistles (Matt. 13:7, 22)
          a. The cares of this world choke out the Word of God
          b. The deceitfulness of riches causes wrong priorities
          c. Idolatry replaces total dedication to the Lord
       2. Fallow ground produces the root of bitterness (Heb. 12:12–15)
          a. We sing of a sweet, sweet spirit in this place
          b. But bitterness often lurks beneath the surface of singing saints
          c. Bitter believers are easily offended and are quick to cause divisions in the church
       3. Fallow ground is often the result of apathy and laziness
          a. Slothful Christians are slow to do what God has commanded (Judg. 18:9)
          b. Slothful Christians hold back from service for the Lord (Prov. 12:27)
          c. Slothful Christians find excuses for not getting involved (Prov. 22:13)
          d. Slothful Christians find that their lives are unproductive (Prov. 24:30)
    C. *How Can Fallow Ground Be Broken Up?*
       1. Fallow ground can be broken up by the plow of God's Word
          a. The Bible is a mirror that enables us to see ourselves as we are (James 1:23)
          b. The Bible also enables us to see ourselves as God sees us
       2. Fallow ground can be broken up by repentance (Rev. 2:4–5)
       3. Fallow ground can be broken up by humility and prayer (2 Chron. 7:14)

III. Conclusion
    A. *What Will It Take to Break Up Your Fallow Ground?*
    B. *Are You Willing to Pray the Price of Revival?*

Successful Farming

Matthew 13:1–8, 18–23

I. **Introduction**
   A. *God Wants to Make Farmers of Us All*
      1. Every believer is the result of someone doing spiritual farming
      2. Sowing and reaping were part of bringing you to Christ
   B. *Christ Told the Parable of the Sower*
      1. Jesus was teaching a multitude by the sea
      2. With a boat for his pulpit, He taught in parables
      3. His first parable had to do with spiritual farming

II. **Body**
   A. *The Sower (v. 3)*
      1. Where is this sower going?
         a. He is going into a field
         b. The world is the field (v. 38)
         c. There is no distinction between "home" and "foreign" missions
      2. What is the importance of this sower's work?
         a. Unless he sows, the field will not produce
         b. Unless he sows, there will be no harvest
      3. How does the sower represent every believer?
         a. We are to go and teach all nations (Matt. 28:18–20)
         b. We are to go into all the world and preach the gospel (Mark 16:15)
         c. We are to be witnesses for Christ until He returns (Acts. 1:8)
   B. *The Seed That Is Sown (v. 4)*
      1. What is this sower sowing?
         a. He is sowing seed in hope of a good harvest
         b. The seed is the Word of God (Luke 8:11)
      2. Why should we sow the Word of God?
         a. Only the Bible has the message that lost sinners need
         b. Only the Bible contains the way of salvation (Acts 4:12)

167

   c. Only the Bible is guaranteed to be effective
    (Isa. 55:11)
  3. How can we sow this good seed?
   a. By living its message before others every day
   b. By telling its message to those we meet along
    the way
   c. By sharing its message through preaching,
    literature, and other media
   d. By bringing others to church where they will
    hear God's Word
  4. Have you done any sowing today?
 C. *The Soil into Which the Seed Is Sown (vv. 4–8)*
  1. He sows by the wayside, where people walk every
   day
  2. He sows in poor soil, where there's little hope of
   growth
  3. He sows among thorns, where the opposition is
   strong
  4. He sows on good soil, where an abundant harvest
   is likely

III. Conclusion
 A. *How Much Sowing Have You Done This Week?*
 B. *Are You Willing to Become a Faithful Sower for the
  Savior?*

Unsuccessful Farming

Ecclesiastes 11:4

I. **Introduction**
   A. *God's Great Plan to Reach the World (Ps. 126:5–6)*
      1. Going and sowing; weeping and reaping
      2. Other references to spiritual farming in the Bible
         a. The parable of the sower (Matt. 13:1–8; 18–23)
         b. Sowing and reaping; labor and wages (John 4:35–38)
   B. *We Are All to Be Sowing and Reaping (Ps. 126:6)*
      1. We are to sow the Word of God and reap souls for Christ
      2. Sowing brings a sense of accomplishment; reaping brings great joy
   C. *A Forecast of Failure for Two Farmers*

II. **Body**
   A. *The Sower Who Would Not Sow*
      1. "He that observeth the wind will not sow"
      2. Here stands a sower who will not sow
         a. He has seeds in his hand but is afraid to drop them into the soil
         b. A harvest awaits if he sows, but he is afraid to do so
      3. The Bible speaks of different kinds of sowing
         a. The sowing of righteous living brings rewards (Prov. 11:18)
         b. The sowing of material wealth brings abundance (2 Cor. 9:6)
         c. The sowing of the Word of God results in reaping souls (Ps. 126:6)
      4. This reluctant sower is immobilized by the wind (the fear of how people will react)
   B. *The Reaper Who Would Not Reap*
      1. "He that regardeth the clouds shall not reap"
      2. This man has sown his seed in spring, and it is time to reap
      3. He stands with scythe in hand but will not swing it
         a. He is afraid to reap because of the clouds

169

        b. He fears that a storm will destroy his long-
awaited crop

        c. His lack of reaping is more deadly than any
predicted storm

    4. Many clouds keep us from reaping

        a. The fear of what people will say if we reap

        b. The fear of beginning well but not being able
to finish

        c. The fear of God's not coming through to help
us reap

    5. "God has not given us the spirit of fear" (2 Tim.
1:7). We can overcome!

  C. *The Harvest That Never Came*

    1. "Shall not reap"

    2. No sowing, no reaping, no harvest

    3. This harvest was lost because of the fear of clouds
and wind

        a. What winds of fear keep you from sowing?

        b. What fearful clouds keep you from reaping?

    4. No harvest of souls for the Savior—how sad!

III. Conclusion

  A. *Clouds and Wind Must Not Prevent a Bountiful
Harvest*

  B. *Fear Must Not Keep Us from Being Faithful*

  C. *Let Us Go and Sow and Weep and Reap, Bringing in
the Harvest*

What Do You Think?

Philippians 4:8

I. Introduction

    A. *Our Thoughts Reveal Who We Are (Prov. 23:7)*

        1. We are not what we think we are

        2. What we think, we are

    B. *Paul Called for Thoughts Centered in Praise (Phil. 4:8)*

        1. He rejects negative, critical thinking as improper for believers

        2. "If there be any virtue, and if there be any praise, think on these things"

II. Body

    A. *Why Our Thought Patterns Are So Important to God*

        1. What we think determines what we say and do

        2. A thought is the father of every word

            a. Every word that brings blessings to others

            b. Every word that inspires and encourages

            c. Every word that discourages and destroys

            d. Every word that cultivates hate and hurt

        3. A thought is the father of every act

            a. Every act of kindness and love

            b. Every act of crime and violence

            c. Every lustful and adulterous act

        4. No wonder God is interested in the topics about which we choose to think

        5. No wonder the psalmist asked the Lord to know his thoughts (Ps. 139:23)

    B. *How We Can Tell If Our Thought Patterns Are Pleasing to God*

        1. Paul summarizes the focus of our thoughts if they are to please God

            a. He gives a picture of the Christian mind as it ought to be

            b. This is what a spiritual MRI of the believer's mind should reveal

        2. Our thoughts should be of things that are true (truthful)

    3. Our thoughts should be of things that are honest (noble)
    4. Our thoughts should be of things that are just (right, good; Acts 10:22)
    5. Our thoughts should be of things that are pure
       a. Not dwelling on the impurity of the times
       b. Calvin: This is "chastity in all departments of life"
    6. Our thoughts should be of things that are lovely and of good report
    7. Our thoughts should be of the best in others
    8. Our thoughts should be focused on praising God

C. *How We Can Conform Our Thought Patterns to God's Will*
    1. Right thoughts come from hearts that are right with God (Ps. 139:23–24)
    2. We must confess our wrong thoughts to the Lord and be forgiven (1 John 1:9)
    3. We must choose mental input that produces good thoughts
       a. What's happening in your devotional life? In your worship of Christ?
       b. How much time do you spend taking in the Bible? In reading Christian books?

III. Conclusion

A. *If Christ Returns Today, What Will He Find on Your Mind?*

B. *What Will You Change to Have Thoughts Pleasing to God?*

C. *Who Will Commit to Developing Thought Patterns of Praise?*

The Scoffers of the Last Days

2 Peter 3:1–4

I. Introduction

   A. *A Book About the Future*

     1. Each chapter in 2 Peter is prophetic

     2. It is an epistle to alert its readers to prepare for the return of Christ

   B. *People Who Scoff at Such Preparation*

     1. They scoff at the prophecies of Christ's return

     2. They scoff at the need for purity in light of Christ's return

     3. They scoff at the promise of Christ's return

   C. *How Shall We Answer These Sarcastic Scoffers?*

II. Body

   A. *Scoffing at the Prophecies of Christ's Return*

     1. Peter reminds us of the words of the prophets (v. 2)

       a. He says that these prophecies are not fables (1:16)

       b. He speaks with authority because he was at the Transfiguration (1:17–18)

       c. The prophets spoke as they were moved by the Holy Spirit (1:21)

     2. David wrote of the Lord's return in power to rule the nations (Ps. 2)

     3. Isaiah wrote of the time when Christ would set up His kingdom (9:6, 7; 11, 35)

     4. Zechariah wrote of the time when we will see the wounded Christ (12:10; 13:6)

     5. The scoffers are themselves a fulfillment of prophesy

       a. Peter said that they would come

       b. Their words in the last days affirm that Christ is coming

   B. *Scoffing at the Need for Purity in Light of Christ's Return*

     1. "Walking after their own lusts"

     2. These scoffers think that morality doesn't matter

      a. They do not expect to stand before our holy God
      b. They think that they can sin and win, but this is impossible (Num. 32:23)
   3. Consider scoffers of the past who were wrong
      a. The scoffers of Noah's time perished in the flood (Gen. 6–7)
      b. The scoffers of Sodom and Gomorrah died in a fiery holocaust (Gen. 19)
      c. Belshazzar, the scoffer, was weighed and found wanting (Dan. 5)
   4. To believers, the return of Christ is a purifying hope (1 John 3:3)
      a. They do not want to be ashamed at the Lord's coming (1 John 2:28)
      b. The imminency of Christ's return calls for holy living (Luke 12:40)
  C. *Scoffing at the Promise of Christ's Coming*
   1. "Where is the promise of his coming?" (v. 4)
   2. There have been many promises of His coming
      a. The signs and promises of Matthew 24:27–44
      b. The warning and promise of Matthew 25:13
      c. The promise of Jesus in the upper room (John 14:1–3)
      d. The promise of Paul to the Thessalonian Christians (1 Thess. 4:13–18)
   3. The long wait for Christ's coming is no reason to doubt that He will come

III. Conclusion
  A. *Turn from Scoffing at Christ to Trusting Him*
  B. *The One You Have Doubted May Return Today*

Why the Long Wait for Christ's Return?

2 Peter 3:9

I. **Introduction**
   A. *Some People Doubt That Christ Will Ever Return (vv. 1–7)*
      1. The long wait seems proof to them that He will not keep His promise
      2. They scoff at the prophecies of His return and live for what feels good
      3. Their poor present judgment will bring them certain future judgment
   B. *Why Has Our Lord Tarried So Long?*
      1. Why has Christ not come to still the voices of the scoffers?
      2. Why has Christ not come to fulfill His promise?
   C. *Peter Gives Some Answers to Those Who Wonder Why We Wait*

II. **Body**
   A. *The Lord's Promise Will Be Fulfilled*
      1. "The Lord is not slack concerning his promise"
      2. Speculating about when Christ will come is fruitless
         a. No one will know in advance (Matt. 24:36)
         b. We can be sure that Christ will return right on time
      3. Each passing moment moves us closer to the fulfillment of the promise
         a. Scoffers cannot change it
         b. Date setters cannot arrange it
         c. It is like a roaring river flowing toward a waterfall
         d. It is like a time bomb ticking off the moments to detonate
      4. God's time is reckoned by His clock, not ours (v. 8)
   B. *The Lord's Patience Has Not Been Exhausted*
      1. The Lord is long-suffering
      2. The patience of God is one of the reasons for His seeming delay

175

3. The psalmist recognized God's patience and gave thanks for it (Ps. 103:8–10)
   a. "The LORD is merciful and gracious, slow to anger, and plenteous in mercy"
   b. We would all be in deep trouble apart from the patience of God
4. Daily reminders of the long-suffering of God
   a. His patience with our prayerlessness
   b. His patience with our lack of concern for souls
   c. His patience with our earthly mindedness
   d. His patience in spite of our inconsistencies
5. Why, then, are we so impatient regarding the fulfillment of His promise?
6. We ought to wait for Christ's coming with confidence and expectation (1 John 2:28)

C. *The Lord's Passion Determines the Arrival of That Great Day*
1. God is "not willing that any should perish"
   a. His promise is predicated on the saving of lost souls
   b. Christ will come when the last soul is won to complete His bride
2. Every day until the Rapture is a call to repentance
3. While time remains, it is time to come to Christ before He comes

III. **Conclusion**
   A. *Turn While There Is Time*
   B. *Today Is the Day of Salvation (2 Cor. 6:1–2)*
   C. *Don't Harden Your Heart and Miss This Opportunity (Heb. 4:7)*

A Text for Tough Times

John 14:1–6

I. Introduction
- A. *Tough Times Come to All*
  1. We all go through things we never thought we would
  2. Many people go through things they didn't think they could
- B. *A Text to Which the Troubled Flee*
  1. The most familiar set of verses in the New Testament
  2. A text for drying tears and giving strength to go on
  3. A favorite text for trembling times
- C. *What Makes This Text So Helpful?*

II. Body
- A. *There Is Comfort Here (v. 1)*
  1. "Let not your heart be troubled"
  2. The world is full of trouble (John 16:33)
     - a. Sickness and pain come to all
     - b. Death visits our families and awaits each of us (Heb. 9:27)
  3. Our Lord wants to comfort those who are going through trouble
     - a. "Comfort ye my people" (Isa. 40:1)
     - b. The God of all comfort (2 Cor. 1:3–4)
  4. Our troubles have not taken God by surprise
     - a. Consider the disciples in the storm on the Sea of Galilee (Mark 4:35–41)
     - b. Jesus is with us in life's storms saying, "Peace, be still" (Mark 4:39)
- B. *There Is a Call to Faith Here (v. 1)*
  1. "Ye believe in God"
  2. "Believe" is a life-changing word
     - a. To believe is to exercise faith
     - b. Believe in Christ and be saved (Acts 16:31)
     - c. Believe and have your prayers answered (Mark 9:23)
  3. "Believe also in me"

        a. Believe that Jesus loves you
        b. Believe that He came to redeem you at the cross
        c. Believe in Him and be sure of heaven

C. *There Is a Question Here (v. 5)*
    1. "How can we know the way?"
    2. Thomas liked what he heard, but he didn't understand
        a. He wanted to go to heaven, but he didn't know how to get there
        b. He wanted to find the formula for eternal life
    3. You may have the same question as Thomas

D. *There Is an Answer Here (v. 6)*
    1. "I am the way, the truth, and the life"
    2. He is not the one who shows the way but the One who IS the way
    3. There is no other way ("no man cometh unto the Father but by me")

III. Conclusion
A. *Jesus Will Meet You Where You Are*
B. *Faith in Christ Will Take You Where He Is*

Too Late

Revelation 22:11–12

I. **Introduction**
   A. *Daniel Was Told to Seal the Book of Prophecy (12:4)*
      1. He had been given insights into the future of empires
      2. He knew the outline of the ages, but certain details were hidden from him
      3. The world wouldn't be ready to understand these details until the time of the end
   B. *John Was Told to Unseal the Book of Prophecy*
      1. Details not known to the prophets would be made clear through him
      2. We live in a time of exciting prophetic fulfillment
      3. Jesus is coming, and it's time to get ready (Rev. 22:7, 12)
   C. *Someday It Will Be Too Late*

II. **Body**
   A. *Too Late for Salvation (v. 11)*
      1. "He that is unjust, let him be unjust still." (We are all unjust in position.)
         a. "There is not a just man upon the earth" (Eccl. 7:20)
         b. "There is none righteous, no, not one" (Rom. 3:10)
         c. "For all have sinned and come short of the glory of God" (Rom. 3:23)
      2. "He that is filthy, let him be filthy still." (We are all filthy in practice.)
         a. Even our good works are but as filthy rags (Isa. 64:6)
         b. How tragic to be unjust and filthy forever
      3. Salvation makes us just and clean (Rom. 5:1; 1 John 1:7)
      4. A day is coming when it will be too late to be saved
   B. *Too Late for Satan (v. 11)*
      1. "He that is righteous, let him be righteous still"

        a. We are made righteous through faith in Christ
(Rom. 4:4)

        b. We are made righteous because of what Christ
did for us (2 Cor. 5:21)

    2. "He that is holy, let him be holy still"

        a. Those who trust in Christ are made holy
(1 Peter 2:9)

        b. They are presented holy before the Lord (Col.
1:22)

    3. Satan tempts us and tries to keep us from holy
living

    4. When Christ comes, all temptation will be over

        a. We will be forever beyond the reach of our
enemy

        b. We will be with the Lord forever, never to be
attacked by Satan again

    5. Satan will finally be in the lake of fire forever
(Rev. 20:10)

  C. *Too Late for Service (v. 12)*

    1. "And behold, I come quickly; and my reward is
with me"

    2. No more time to reach loved ones and neighbors
for Christ

    3. No more time to earn rewards for service for Christ

        a. Christ will come, and rewards will be given

        b. This is the time to serve; someday it will be
too late

III. Conclusion

  A. *Come to Christ to Be Saved Before It Is Too Late*

  B. *Give Your All in Serving Christ Before It Is Too Late*

    1. Warn your world of the shortness of time before it
is too late

    2. Invest your life in winning souls before it is too
late

Thankful for What?

Thanksgiving   *Psalm 103:2*

I. Introduction
   A. *David's Great Song of Thanksgiving*
      1. He encourages himself to give thanks for daily blessings
      2. He reminds himself of the many benefits God has given him
   B. *The Pilgrims Remembered God's Benefits*
      1. They arrived November 11, 1620, on the rocky coast of Cape Cod
      2. They came to the New World to seek a place to worship in freedom
      3. They suffered many hardships the first winter, including the deaths of half of them
      4. They established the first Thanksgiving in spite of their many problems
   C. *For What Should We Be Thankful?*

II. Body
   A. *We Should Be Thankful for the Essentials of Life (1 Tim. 6:8)*
      1. Having food should make us thankful
         a. A good harvest made the Pilgrims thankful; they had little else
         b. Millions of people go to bed hungry; enough to eat is cause for thanksgiving
      2. Having adequate clothing should make us thankful
         a. Winter finds many people cold and insufficiently protected
         b. Those who are comfortably clothed are a privileged few
      3. What other essentials do we take for granted?
      4. Let's focus on what we have instead of what we want—and be thankful for it
   B. *We Should Be Thankful for Everything in Life (1 Thess. 5:18)*
      1. All things work together for the good of those who love God (Rom. 8:28)

2. Our loving Father has the whole world in His
hands
   a. Be thankful for His weather, whatever it may
   be
   b. Be thankful for His promises that meet us in
   life's storms
   c. Be thankful that we know the One who holds
   the future and can rest in His care
3. Be thankful that there is a design in our difficulties
   a. Trouble teaches us patient trust in the Lord
   (Rom. 5:3)
   b. Problems large and small are intended to make
   us more like Jesus (Rom. 8:29)
4. Be thankful for trouble that has *not* come our way
   a. God spares us many heartaches of which we
   are unaware
   b. He delivers us from destruction (v. 4)

C. *We Should Be Thankful for Eternal Life (2 Cor. 9:15)*
   1. God's grace should make us thankful
      a. We are all sinners, undeserving of salvation
      (Rom. 3:10–23)
      b. We deserve only death and hell (Rom. 6:23)
      c. The gift of His grace is eternal life (Rom. 6:23;
      Eph. 2:8–9)
   2. We who were without hope have been assured that
   we'll never perish (John 3:16)
   3. Assurance of eternal life should make us thankful
   every day (1 John 5:12–13)

III. **Conclusion**
   A. *Christians Will Be Thankful in Heaven (Rev. 7:11)*
   B. *Start Rehearsing Heaven's Song of Thanksgiving*
   C. *A Thankful Heart Will Make Earth More Heavenly*

Thanksgiving in Stocks and Bonds

Thanksgiving   *Acts 16:23–34*

I. **Introduction**
   A. *Many People Invest in Stocks and Bonds*
      1. They have invested in hope of financial gain
      2. Their futures rest on their investments
      3. Their moods rise and fall with the markets
   B. *Paul and Silas Had Made More Lasting Investments*
      1. They had sold out to their Savior
      2. They had invested their lives in His service, expecting eternal dividends
      3. They had stocks and bonds in a Philippian prison
   C. *How Could These Persecuted Preachers Be Thankful?*

II. **Body**
   A. *They Were Thankful for What God Had Done*
      1. "At midnight, Paul and Silas prayed and sang praises" (v. 25)
         a. They praised God because He had saved them from sin
         b. They praised God for what had made salvation possible
      2. How could they praise God after being beaten for their faith? (v. 23)
         a. They remembered that Christ had been beaten for them
         b. He had been wounded and bruised as prophesied (Isa. 53)
      3. Like Jesus, they had been imprisoned for doing good
      4. They might face death, but they remembered that Jesus had faced the cross
      5. Their prison cell was dark, but Jesus had died for them on dark Calvary
   B. *They Were Thankful for What God Was Doing*
      1. They knew that God was at work in their lives (Phil. 1:6)
      2. They knew that God had called them to this place (Acts 16:9)

183

      3. They had witnessed conversions as a result of being there (v. 14)

      4. They had seen the demon-possessed fortune teller delivered (v. 18)

      5. They could then be thankful, knowing that they were in God's will

         a. Are you thankful for where you are?

         b. Even if you are going through troubled times?

      6. Two life-changing options

         a. We can focus on what God is doing and be thankful

         b. We can focus on what the devil is doing and be miserable

  C. *They Were Thankful for What God Was Going to Do*

      1. They prayed and believed

         a. We can pray and believe and receive

         b. We can pray and doubt and go without

      2. God rewarded their praying and praising in stocks and bonds

         a. The earth quaked, the prison doors opened, and they were free

         b. God is going to do wonderful things for all believers (Phil. 1:20–23; 3:2–21)

III. Conclusion

  A. *How Two Thankful Preachers Brought Others to Christ*

      1. The jailer and his family came to faith in Christ (vv. 27–34)

      2. Others also believed and met with Paul and Silas to rejoice (v. 40)

  B. *Thankful Living Can Bring Others to Eternal Life*

New Things for Nathanael

John 1:43–51

I. **Introduction**
   A. *Getting Acquainted with a Little-Known Bible Character*
      1. Nathanael was in contrast to Peter, James, and John
      2. Nathanael has a lot in common with most of us
   B. *What Was Going On?*
      1. Jesus was beginning His earthly ministry
      2. He was gathering His disciples
   C. *What Brought About Nathanael's New Life?*

II. **Body**
   A. *A Seeking Savior (vv. 43–44)*
      1. Jesus found Philip and said, "Follow me"
      2. Our Lord is a seeking Savior
         a. He is like the sower who went forth to sow good seed (Matt. 13:3)
         b. He is like the shepherd who went seeking lost sheep (Luke 15:4–10)
         c. He is like the prodigal son's father, who longed for His son's return (Luke 15:11–32)
      3. This is the neglected part of the character of Christ in too many churches
         a. We have made Christ a therapist rather than a Savior
         b. We have made Christ a politician rather than a Savior
         c. We have made Christ a solution for success rather than a Savior
         d. We have made Christ a master motivator rather than a Savior
      4. We must return to the message of the Savior who seeks lost souls
   B. *A Seeking Saved One (vv. 45–46)*
      1. "Philip findeth Nathanael"
         a. Philip had an immediate interest in souls
         b. Following Christ calls for reaching lost ones
      2. Evangelism is an evidence that salvation is real

185

         a.   New converts often win more souls than older believers in the churches

         b.   Following Jesus results in bringing others to Him (Matt. 4:19)

     3.   Philip's mistaken but effective witness

         a.   He called Jesus the son of Joseph

         b.   The Lord often uses us in spite of our ignorance when we care for souls

     4.   Philip's bringing Nathanael to Jesus is a good example for us all

C. *A Saved Sinner (vv. 46–49)*

     1.   Nathanael was skeptical: "Can any good thing come out of Nazareth?"

         a.   Skepticism is a normal first reaction to the gospel

         b.   How Philip overcame Nathanael's skepticism: "Come and see"

         c.   An ounce of testimony is worth a pound of argument

     2.   Nathanael was surprised: "Whence knowest thou me?"

         a.   Jesus had called him by name; He knows us before we know Him

         b.   Jesus told Nathanael about himself; He knows all about us

     3.   Nathanael was satisfied: "Thou art the Son of God"

III. Conclusion

A. *Great and New Things Were Ahead for Nathanael (vv. 50–51)*

B. *Receiving Christ as Savior Will Make Things New for You*

New Desires for New People

Ephesians 2:13–15; Acts 8:36;
1 Peter 2:2; 1 John 3:14

I. **Introduction**
   A. *The Christian Life Begins with a New Birth*
      1. Religious Nicodemus was told that he must be born again (John 3:3–7)
      2. This new birth results from faith in Christ (John 3:16)
      3. A new life is made possible by the death of Christ on the cross
         a. We are brought near to God by the blood of Christ (Eph. 2:13)
         b. Trusting Christ as Savior makes all things new (Eph. 2:15; 2 Cor. 5:17)
   B. *New People Have New Desires*
      1. Things they once desired hold no interest for them anymore
      2. What do these newborn ones desire?

II. **Body**
   A. *They Desire Baptism (Acts 8:36)*
      1. Philip led an important Ethiopian to Christ
         a. He helped him see that Isaiah had prophesied the cross
         b. He brought him to faith in the One who died and rose again for him
      2. The new convert's question: "What doth hinder me to be baptized?"
      3. All converts in the New Testament church were baptized
      4. Baptism publicly identifies born again believers with the Savior
         a. Baptism proclaims the gospel to onlookers
         b. Baptism is obedience to Christ (Matt. 28:18–20)
      5. What hinders you from being baptized?
   B. *They Desire the Bible (1 Peter 2:2)*
      1. "Desire the sincere milk of the word"
         a. The Bible plays a vital role in the new birth (1:23)

187

       b. The Bible contains the vitamins of spiritual health

       c. The Bible causes growth ("that ye may grow thereby")

  2. The new birth opens our eyes to biblical truth (1 Cor. 2:14)

  3. The Bible is God's great detergent that cleans up our lives

       a. "How shall a young man cleanse his way?" (Ps. 119:9–11)

       b. "Now ye are clean through the word" (John 15:3)

       c. "The washing of water by the word" (Eph. 5:26)

  4. New people want to live victorious lives

       a. We overcome temptation by using the Bible (Matt. 4:1–11)

       b. The Bible gives us victory over satanic powers (Eph. 6:17)

C. *They Desire the Body (1 John 3:14)*

  1. "We love the brethren"

  2. The early Christians had wonderful fellowship (Acts 2:41–45)

  3. "The fellowship of kindred minds is like to that above"

  4. We are all members of the same body (1 Cor. 12:12–14)

  5. Something is wrong when professing Christians don't desire to be with other believers

III. Conclusion

A. *Are You Sure That You Have Been Born Again?*

B. *Are the Biblical Desires of Born-Again People Found in You?*

C. *Examine Yourself to See if You Are in the Faith (2 Cor. 13:5)*

December
The Other Miracle Birth

Christmas Series Begins   *Luke 1:5–13; 3:1–22; 7:18–28*

I. Introduction
A. *The Countdown to Christmas*
B. *The Other Countdown*
   1. The world had awaited a Savior for centuries
   2. The prophets had spoken of a miracle birth
      a. The Savior was to be born of a virgin (Isa. 7:14)
      b. The eternal One was to enter time at Bethlehem (Mic. 5:2)
C. *The Prophecy of Another Miracle Birth*
   1. One was to be born who would prepare for the coming of the Savior (Isa. 40)
   2. John the Baptist was not born of a virgin, but his birth was a miracle (Luke 1:5–13)

II. Body
A. *The Parents of John the Baptist (vv. 5–13)*
   1. Zacharias and Elisabeth had no children and were up in years
      a. Zacharias was a priest during the reign of Herod
      b. Elisabeth was a descendent of Aaron
   2. The announcement came in the temple
      a. Gabriel came to Zacharias while he was serving in the temple
      b. God meets us while we're serving; Satan meets us when we're idle
   3. Zacharias was afraid and had trouble believing the angel's message (v. 12)
   4. The father of "the voice" lost his voice because of his unbelief
   5. John was born as Gabriel promised and was Spirit filled from birth
B. *The Preaching of John the Baptist (3:1–22)*
   1. John came to prepare the way of the Lord (Isa. 40:3–8)

189

  2. This preparation meant preaching repentance (Luke 3:3–9)

   a. John boldly named sins and confronted evil

   b. We must face our sins, or we will not flee to Christ for forgiveness

  3. John pointed to Christ as the sin bearer, "the Lamb of God" (John 1:29)

  4. John called Christ the bridegroom (John 3:29)

  5. John humbled himself and exalted Christ (Luke 3:16)

  6. John's plain preaching cost him his freedom (Luke 3:17–20)

   a. He warned his hearers of judgment to come

   b. He played no favorites, rebuking even Herod for immorality

 C. *Our Lord's Praise of John the Baptist (7:19–28)*

  1. John's surprising question: "Art thou he that should come?"

   a. He asked this question from prison with his life in jeopardy

   b. Depression drives us to foolish questions and conclusions

  2. Our Lord's faith-building answer: His miracles proved His deity (v. 22)

  3. Jesus affirmed that John was God's messenger (vv. 24–30)

   a. Vance Havner writes, "When John said his worst, Jesus said His best about John."

   b. "There is not a greater prophet than John the Baptist"

III. Conclusion

 A. *John's Message Still Prepares the Way of the Lord*

 A. *Hear the Call of John the Baptist: "Repent!"*

 B. *Heed the Call of Jesus: "Come unto Me . . . I Will Give You Rest"*

Fear Not, Joseph

I. **Introduction**
   A. *The "Fear Nots" of Christmas*
      1. A "fear not" for Zacharias (Luke 1:13)
      2. A "fear not" for Mary (Luke 1:30)
      3. A "fear not" for the shepherds (Luke 2:10)
   B. *Joseph Needed A "Fear Not"*
      1. Everything had been going so well for him
         a. He was engaged to the girl of his dreams
         b. They were making plans for their future
      2. Then he discovered that Mary was with child
      3. Suddenly his world came crashing down; he was afraid of the future
   C. *Some "Fear Nots" for Times When We Feel Like Joseph*

II. **Body**
   A. *A "Fear Not" for Times When We've Been Let Down (v. 18)*
      1. Joseph concluded that Mary had been immoral
         a. We often come to wrong conclusions about what's going on
         b. No wonder Jesus warned against judging others (Matt. 7:1)
      2. While Joseph was worrying, God was working out a wonderful plan for his life
      3. Mary had not been immoral; she was the prophesied virgin with child (Isa. 7:14)
      4. What Joseph had thought was sinful was sacred; he didn't have all the facts
      5. We must stop fretting about the failures of others; God is in control (Ps. 37:1–4)
   B. *A "Fear Not" for Times When We Worry About Public Opinion (v. 19)*
      1. Joseph was not willing to make Mary a public example
         a. He didn't want Mary to be destroyed for her supposed sin

      b.   He feared what others would do when the facts were known

  2. Joseph was allowing public opinion to shape his future

      a.   Our responsibility is to do what God wants us to do

      b.   The fear of public opinion can keep us from God's best

      c.   "The fear of man bringeth a snare" (Prov. 29:25)

  3. Those who are in the center of God's will do not need to fear public reaction

  4. Are you afraid to surrender to Christ for fear of what others will say or do?

C. *A "Fear Not" for Times of Mental Anguish (v. 20)*

  1. "But while he thought on these things"

      a.   He must have thought on these things continually

      b.   Imagine Joseph's state of mind during this emotional crisis

  2. Joseph's anxiety was without foundation

      a.   What he thought would bring death brought deliverance

      b.   What he thought would ruin Mary's name immortalized it

      c.   He thought that people would call Mary bad; instead, they call her blessed

  3. Many of our fears are groundless; we need to exchange our fears for faith

III. Conclusion

A. *Do You Need a "Fear Not" Today?*

B. *God Will Meet You in Your Fears as He Met Joseph*

C. *Cast All Your Cares on the One Who Cares for You (1 Peter 5:7)*

Christmas Gifts Yet to Come

Christmas Series   *Luke 1:32–33; Isaiah 9:6–7*

I. **Introduction**
  A. *The Birth of Christ Fulfilled Many Prophecies*
      1. The converging of specific prophecies when Christ was born
      2. The virgin birth (Isa. 7:14), the birth in Bethlehem (Mic. 5:2), etc.
  B. *Gabriel Brought a Wonderful Message to Mary*
      1. She had found favor with God
      2. She would conceive as a virgin and bear the Savior
      3. Her son would be great and be called the Son of the Highest
  C. *Fulfilled Christmas Prophecies Have Been Great Gifts to Us*
  D. *What About the Christmas Prophecies That Are Unfulfilled?*

II. **Body**
  A. *Christ Hasn't Yet Occupied the Throne of David (v. 32)*
      1. Christ is called the Son of God, as promised by Gabriel
          a. Millions of people have received the Son of God by faith and found Him true
          b. Receiving this gift brings assurance of salvation (1 John 5:12–13)
      2. But Christ will finally occupy the throne of David
          a. The prophets looked forward to the fulfillment of this prophecy (Isa. 11)
          b. Gabriel gave this promise to Mary (v. 32)
      3. The wise men came seeking the King of the Jews (Matt. 2:2)
      4. John the Baptist came announcing the coming of the kingdom of heaven
      5. Until Christ is on David's throne, let Him be on the throne of your heart
  B. *Christ Hasn't Yet Established His Earthly Kingdom (Isa. 9:6)*
      1. "And the government shall be upon his shoulder"

    2. Jesus taught His disciples to pray for His coming kingdom (Matt. 6:9–10)

    3. The disciples looked forward to the establishing of Christ's kingdom (Acts 1:6–7)

        a. They were still looking forward to this after the resurrection

        b. Peter preached about the Lord's coming kingdom (Acts 3:19–21)

    4. Paul wrote to Timothy concerning the Lord's coming kingdom (2 Tim. 4:1)

    5. John described the coming of the King of Kings to reign (Rev. 19:11–16)

        a. Christ will then rule the nations

        b. Believers will rule with Him (Rev. 20:6)

    6. What a wonderful gift this will be to all the world!

  C. *Christ Hasn't Yet Brought Justice to the Earth (Isa. 9:7)*

    1. "To establish it with judgment and with justice"

    2. The angels promised the shepherds peace on earth (Luke 2:14)

        a. Those who trust Christ as Savior find personal peace (Phil. 4:6–8)

        b. But wars and wrongs remain throughout the earth

    3. Injustice is common to all nations. What's wrong? When will this change?

        a. Christ has been rejected as Savior, Lord, and King

        b. He will return and bring peace and justice to the world

III. Conclusion

  A. *The Promises of Prophets and Angels Will Be Fulfilled*

  B. *The King Is Coming to Bring Peace to This Troubled World*

  C. *Troubled Hearts Can Find Peace Through Faith in Him Today*

Christmas Communion

Christmas Series   *Luke 2:7; 22:19–20*

I. **Introduction**
   A. *Christmas and Communion Are About Giving*
      1. It is the season for giving
      2. God is the great Giver
         a. The Giver of life (Gen. 2:7)
         b. The Giver of all good things (James 1:17)
      3. Communion is about the greatest gift of all (John 3:16)
         a. Those who have received this gift can take communion
         b. They do so remembering the gift of Christ to bring salvation
   B. *What Did Christ Give That Is So Important?*

II. **Body**
   A. *Christ Gave His Body (2:7; 22:19)*
      1. "This is my body which is given for you"
      2. The prophets wrote of God's taking a body
         a. He would be born of a virgin (Isa. 7:14)
         b. The everlasting One would enter time in Bethlehem (Mic. 5:2)
         c. The omnipresent Lord would limit Himself to a body
      3. "And she brought forth her firstborn son"
      4. Paul called this event God's becoming man (Phil. 2:5–7)
      5. At Christmas, we celebrate Christ's taking a body
      6. In communion, we celebrate Christ's giving His body on the cross
   B. *Christ Gave His Blood (22:20)*
      1. "This cup is the new testament in my blood"
         a. "Which is shed for you"
         b. The first communion announced the new covenant
      2. "She wrapped him in swaddling clothes"
         a. These were the baby clothes of the poor
         b. They were also the clothing of the dead

   3. This child was born to die
      a. Mary laid the babe in a manger
      b. It was a fitting place to lay the Lamb of God
      c. He would be the sacrifice for sin (Heb. 10:4–10)
   4. Peter wrote of the redeeming precious blood of Christ (1 Peter 1:19)
   5. John wrote of the blood that cleanses from all sin (1 John 1:7)

  C. *Christ Gave His Best (22:20)*
   1. He was always about His Father's business
   2. When tempted, He was steadfast and victorious
   3. When suffering, He neither complained nor threatened
   4. When dying, He was faithful and in control to the end

III. Conclusion
  A. *Now It Is Our Turn to Give*
   1. What can we give the One who gave His all?
   2. We can give Him our hearts and our lives for His service (Rom. 12:1–2)
  B. *What Will You Give the Christ of the Manger and the Cross?*

The Night Shepherds Became Missionaries

Christmas Series   *Luke 2:7–18*

I. **Introduction**
   A. *The Hour of the Ages*
      1. History had been waiting for the hour of Christ's birth
      2. The words of the prophets had been waiting fulfillment for centuries
      3. When Mary gave birth to Jesus, the long-awaited hour had arrived
   B. *Witnesses Called to Confirm This Holy Historic Event*
      1. Angels were dispatched to a nearby hillside to announce the birth of Christ
      2. Shepherds were invited to Bethlehem's manger to see the newborn Savior
      3. Imagine being with the shepherds on this night of miracles

II. **Body**
   A. *The Night (v. 8)*
      1. The first announcement of Christ's birth was at night
      2. How fitting that Christ should be born at night!
         a. The world was in spiritual darkness
         b. Christ was born to deliver those in the darkness of sin (Rom. 13:12–13)
         c. The birth that night would doom the powers of darkness (Eph. 6:12–18)
      3. What night meant to the shepherds until the angels came
         a. Night was a time of weariness and worry over their sheep
         b. Night was the end of another day of unfulfilled ambitions
         c. Night was a time of uncertainty over what might happen as they slept
      4. Then an angelic announcement of salvation changed everything

B. *The Light (v. 9)*
1. Suddenly, the hillside was flooded with light
   a. The glory of the Lord shone round about them
   b. The darkness in their lives was about to flee away
2. Light and the Lord
   a. The first words of creation were "Let there be light" (Gen. 1:3)
   b. "The Lord is my light and my salvation" (Ps. 27:1)
   c. "In him was life; and the life was the light of men" (John 1:4)
3. The One in the manger would say, "I am the light of the world" (John 8:12)
4. Christ came to call us out of darkness into His marvelous light (1 Peter 2:9)
5. Believers are headed for heaven, where the Lamb is the light (Rev. 21:23)

C. *Their Fright (vv. 9–11)*
1. "They were sore afraid"
2. The light of God reveals His holiness and our sinfulness (Isa. 6:1–8)
3. The angelic message took their fears away
   a. "Fear not; for, behold, I bring you good tidings of great joy"
   b. The message was of a Savior, "who is Christ the Lord"
4. Faith in Christ takes our fears—and our sins—away

III. Conclusion

A. *Faith Was Turned to Sight (vv. 15–17)*
1. The shepherds went to Bethlehem and found their promised Savior
2. After seeing Jesus, they became the first missionaries, telling others of Him
B. *Christmas Should Move Us to Be Missionaries Too*

Angels After Christmas

Christmas Series   *Matthew 2:11–13, 19–20*

I. **Introduction**
  A. *The Current Interest in Angels*
    1. Good if the information on angels is presented as in the Bible
    2. Harmful if the teaching about angels is not biblical
  B. *Biblical Facts About Angels*
    1. They are created beings who do not marry or reproduce (Mark 12:25)
    2. People do not become angels at death (Mark 12:25)
    3. They are masculine in appearance (Acts. 1:10)
    4. They have masculine names (note Gabriel and Michael)
    5. They are messengers of God ministering to believers (Heb. 1:14)
  C. *Angels: Active Reporters of the Birth of Christ*
  D. *The Work of Angels After Christmas*

II. **Body**
  A. *They Were Protectors (Matt. 2:12–13)*
    1. Herod had told the wise men to report their findings to him
      a. He wanted to destroy Jesus
      b. The wise men were warned to depart another way
    2. An angel told Joseph to flee into Egypt
      a. This event is Exodus in reverse
      b. This event was to fulfill the Scriptures
    3. Angels protect those who trust the Savior today
  B. *They Were Directors (2:19–20)*
    1. After Herod died, it was safe to return
    2. Joseph had to be notified
      a. An angel appeared to him in a dream
      b. This situation was similar to the announcement to Joseph of Christ's coming birth
    3. Angels have often directed believers who needed God's guidance

        a. Angels directed Lot to depart from doomed Sodom (Gen. 19)

        b. An angel directed Daniel concerning coming prophetic events (Dan. 12)

    4. The direction of angels is always consistent with the Word of God

  C. *They Were Encouragers (4:11)*

    1. Angels encouraged Jesus following His encounter with Satan (Matt. 4)

        a. His temptation in the desert had left Him drained and strained

        b. Even Jesus needed encouragement

    2. We can all do the work of angels by encouraging the people we meet daily

  D. *They Were Announcers (28:2; Acts 1:10–11)*

    1. Angels were not summoned to the cross

    2. Christ could have called twelve legions of angels to set Him free

    3. Their responsibility was to announce Christ's resurrection and return

    4. We are also to make these great announcements to the world (Matt. 28:18–20)

III. Conclusion

  A. *Believers Share Some of the Responsibilities of Angels*

  B. *Angels Complete Their Assignments—Will We?*

Why the Christ of Christmas Must Return

Christmas Series   *Luke 1:67–79*

I. **Introduction**
   A. *All of the Promises of the Prophets Must Be Fulfilled*
      1. Many prophecies about Jesus were fulfilled in His birth in Bethlehem
      2. Many prophecies about Jesus were fulfilled in His death and resurrection
      3. But some prophecies about Jesus remain unfulfilled
   B. *We Have Many Promises That Christ Will Return*
      1. The promise of Jesus (John 14:3)
      2. The promise of angels (Acts 1:10–11)
      3. The promise of Paul (1 Thess. 4:13–18)
   C. *Why Must Christ Return?*

II. **Body**
   A. *Christ Must Return to Complete His Work in the Nations*
      1. The Scriptures concerning His work in the nations must be fulfilled
      2. The prophets wrote of His atoning work
         a. Wrote of His death (Ps. 22; Isa. 53)
         b. Wrote of His resurrection (Ps. 16:10–11)
      3. The prophets also wrote of His coming Kingdom
         a. These prophecies had to do with Israel and other nations
         b. Many of these prophecies of His Kingdom are not fulfilled
      4. Zacharias prophesied the conquest of Israel's enemies (Luke 1:70–74)
      5. Christ must return to fulfill these promises to Israel and other nations
   B. *Christ Must Return to Complete His Work in Nature*
      1. Christ exercised authority over nature during His ministry
         a. He stilled the raging sea (Mark 4:39)
         b. He walked on water (John 6:19)
         c. He rode an unbroken colt (Luke 19:30)

201

   2. Christ exercised authority over nature in His death
     a. The sun was darkened (Matt. 27:45)
     b. There was a great earthquake (Matt. 27:51)
   3. When Christ returns to establish His kingdom, the earth will be fruitful (Isa. 35:1)
   4. When Christ returns, the desert will blossom as a rose (Isa. 35:1)
  C. *Christ Must Return to Complete His Work in New Believers*
   1. Christ begins a good work in us at conversion (Phil. 1:6)
     a. We are made new creatures (2 Cor. 5:17)
     b. The Holy Spirit takes up residence in us (1 Cor. 6:19)
     c. We embark on God's great plan for our lives (Rom. 8:28)
   2. We are not yet what we ought to be
     a. We are still works in progress
     b. God is not through with us yet
   3. When Christ returns, we will be like Him (1 John 3:2)

III. Conclusion
  A. *The Christ of Christmas Is Coming Again*
  B. *He's Preparing Us for That Great Day*
  C. *Are You Ready for Christ's Return?*

Let's Celebrate Salvation

Christmas Series Ends   *1 Peter 1:10–12*

I. **Introduction**
   A. *We Have Just Celebrated the Birth of the Savior*
      1. Have we given enough attention to salvation?
      2. We did not celebrate the birth of a philosopher but of a Savior
      3. Any celebration of the Savior must include celebrating salvation
   B. *We Must Get Back to the Basics*
      1. All men are sinners and need to be saved (Rom. 3:10–23)
      2. Jesus came to save sinners (Luke 19:10)
   C. *Why Celebrate Salvation?*

II. **Body**
   A. *Let's Celebrate Because Christ Has Put Away the Past*
      1. What good news this is at the end of the year!
         a. Television news reports summarize the past year
         b. Newspapers publish extensive articles doing the same
         c. What if these events summarized your life?
      2. Are there things you would like to omit from the year's replay?
      3. When we come to Christ, the past is forgiven
         a. The sins of the past are all gone at last
         b. All of the failures of our past are forgotten
      4. Salvation brings not only forgiveness but also justification
      5. Subject your sins to these past erasers: Psalm 103:3; Isaiah 1:16; 1 John 1:9
   B. *Let's Celebrate Because Christ Is with Us in the Present*
      1. The prophets marveled about salvation by grace
         a. They had difficulty understanding such love
         b. How could breakers of God's laws be forgiven?

203

    2. Angels wanted to know more about salvation by grace
        a. God's amazing grace must have increased their joy in announcing Christ's birth
        b. How could these sinners be made part of the family of God?
        c. How could these former lost ones be partakers of God's nature?
    3. The Savior will never leave us (Heb. 13:5–6)
    4. We will not face the new year alone
    5. Christ is with us right now

C. *Let's Celebrate Because Christ Will Be with Us in the Future*
    1. The best is yet to come
    2. Present suffering cannot be compared with the coming glory (Rom. 8:18)
    3. Christ is with us now, and heaven is ahead
    4. Even death cannot steal our hope for the future (Phil. 1:20–23)
        a. John Wesley on his deathbed: "Best of all, God is with us."
        b. The future is as bright as the promises of God

III. Conclusion
A. *Do You Have This Great Salvation?*
    1. Face the question honestly
    2. Don't settle for less than a "know so salvation"
B. *When You Know You've Been Born Again . . . Celebrate!*

It's Dynamite

Romans 1:14–16

I. Introduction
A. *Paul Was in Debt (v. 14)*
1. He considered himself in debt to everyone
   a. The Greeks and the barbarians
   b. The wise and the unwise
2. He was in debt because he had received the gospel
3. He was discharging his debt by preaching the gospel
B. *Christ Was the Driving Force in Paul's Life (v. 15)*
1. So, as much as in me is—not holding back anything
2. All his energy invested in reaching people for Christ

II. Body
A. *Paul Was Not Ashamed of the Gospel (v. 16)*
1. What is the gospel? (1 Cor. 15:3–4)
   a. Christ died for our sins according to the Scriptures
   b. He was buried and rose again according to the Scriptures
2. We should not be ashamed to share this good news
3. Too many believers are ashamed of the gospel
   a. Ashamed to tell others of Christ and His love
   b. Ashamed to seize opportunities to witness
4. Are you ashamed to share your faith with lost people?
5. How can we be ashamed of Jesus when He has endured our shame on the cross?
B. *Paul Was Amazed at the Power of the Gospel (v. 16)*
1. "It is the power of God unto salvation"
2. What the gospel accomplishes
   a. It saves souls from death (Rom. 6:23)
   b. It offers hope to lost sinners
   c. It brings about the new birth when it is received
   d. It makes all things new in believers (2 Cor. 5:17)

        e.   It succeeds when human wisdom fails (1 Cor. 1:18)

    3.   The gospel is the dynamite of God, changing lives and bringing eternal life

C. *Paul Was Astonished at the Availability of the Gospel (v. 16)*

    1.   Paul was a Jew and had thought that salvation must be for Jews only

        a.   He had been proud of his heritage (Phil. 3:1–14)

        b.   He had been a persecutor of Christians (Acts. 9:1–9)

        c.   He considered himself the chief of sinners (1 Tim. 1:15)

        d.   Still, he discovered that the gospel message could save him

    2.   Now he knew that the gospel was for all people

        a.   Jews and Gentiles, rich and poor (Rom. 10:9–13)

        b.   The down and out and the up and out (Heb. 7:25)

    3.   Paul was thrilled with the "whosoever" of the gospel invitation

III.   Conclusion

A.   *A Call to Those Who Need to Respond to the Gospel*

B.   *A Call to Those Who Have Been Ashamed of the Gospel*

C.   *A Call to All Believers to Share the Gospel*

Let's Stop Contradicting God

Ephesians 6:1–3; Jeremiah 31:3;
Luke 1:37; 1 Corinthians 10:13

I. **Introduction**
   A. *Children Sometimes Contradict Their Parents*
      1. This is a distressingly common occurrence
      2. Contradicting is rebellion and an offense to God
   B. *Many Believers Contradict Their Heavenly Father*
      1. Our Father always speaks the truth
      2. Contradicting God is rebelling against the truth
   C. *Let's Look at Some Examples of Contradicting God*

II. **Body**
   A. *"God Doesn't Love Me" (Jer. 31:3)*
      1. "I have loved thee with an everlasting love"
      2. The gospel declares God's love for us all
         a. The birth of Christ in Bethlehem's stable proves God's love
         b. The compassionate miracles of Christ prove God's love (John 11:35–44)
         c. The sufferings of Christ on the cross prove God's love (Isa. 53)
         d. The forgiveness of Christ proves God's love (Luke 23:34)
         e. The death of Christ for sinners proves God's love (John 15:13)
         f. The resurrection of Christ as promised proves God's love (John 10:15–18)
      3. God's love is seen in His creation
      4. God's love is seen in His plan of redemption
      5. How can anyone doubt God's love?
   B. *"It's Impossible" (Luke 1:37)*
      1. "For with God nothing shall be impossible"
      2. Gabriel's promise to Mary has always been true
      3. Israel doubted God's power at the Red Sea (Exod. 14)
         a. Pharaoh's armies were behind them and approaching fast

207

       b. The Red Sea was ahead of them, and they had no boats

       c. God had promised safe passage, but it seemed impossible (14:14)

       d. The Red Sea opened, and Israel went through on dry ground

    4. The disciples doubted in a raging storm on the Sea of Galilee

       a. High winds and waves threatened to take their lives

       b. The boat was taking on water and about to go down

       c. "Carest thou not that we perish?" the disciples asked (Mark 4:38)

       d. Jesus arose and rebuked the sea, and there was a great calm

    5. We often pray as if we think that God can't come through in the tough times

    6. Let's stop doubting and contradicting and start believing

  C. *"I Can't Overcome This Temptation" (1 Cor. 10:13)*

    1. God limits our temptations to "such as is common to man"

    2. God is faithful to His tempted children

    3. God limits our temptations to what we can overcome

    4. God is faithful and provides a way to escape from every temptation

III. Conclusion

  A. *We Must Stop Being Disobedient to Our Heavenly Father*

  B. *We Must Stop Contradicting God and Start Trusting Him*

A Promise for All Seasons

Romans 8:28

I. Introduction
 A. *A Text That Meets Where We Live*
  1. A promise that raises the hopes of troubled people
  2. A guarantee that God has a plan for each of His children
 B. *Not an Easy Promise to Remember When Times Are Tough*
  1. We may be overwhelmed by difficulties
  2. We may think that God has forgotten us
  3. We may think that our lives are out of control
 C. *A Promise That Faith Can Claim and Find Peace*

II. Body
 A. *A Promise That Brings Assurance*
  1. "And we know"
  2. God wants to replace our uncertainty with faith
  3. The uncertainty of the unbeliever
   a. Doesn't know why he is here
   b. Doesn't know how life began
   c. Doesn't know what life is all about
   d. Doesn't know where he will be after death
  4. Faith in Christ trades uncertainty for assurance
  5. "I know whom I have believed" (2 Tim. 1:12)
  6. "These things are written that ye might know" (1 John 5:13)
 B. *A Promise About All the Experiences of Life*
  1. "All things work together for good"
  2. Some experiences are hard to bear
   a. We experience things that shake or break us
   b. We experience things that we can't understand
  3. How God brings good out of difficult circumstances
   a. Moses: a fugitive who became a deliverer
   b. Joseph: His brothers sold him but God sent him
   c. Margaret Clarkson: lived in pain but blessed many

      d. Annie Johnson Flint: "He giveth more grace"
      e. Fanny Crosby: blind, but her songs minister to millions

C. *A Promise About a Wonderful Plan for Believers*
  1. "To them that love God"
  2. This begins with God's love for us (Rom. 5:8)
    a. We respond to this love by faith in Christ
    b. "We love Him because He first loved us" (1 John 4:19)
  3. God works out His plan for His children
    a. He brings good out of bad experiences
    b. He rewards sufferers beyond their expectations

III. Conclusion
  A. *Are You Hurting? Down? Depressed?*
  B. *Rest on God's Promise for All Seasons*
    George Burns states, "Suffering saints live and move in the heart of a divine conspiracy of love."

Why Feel Guilty?

Psalm 32:3–5

I. **Introduction**
  A. *David's Description of His Guilt Feelings*
     1. He feels miserable and unhappy all day long
     2. Can you identify with the guilty king?
  B. *What Is Guilt?*
     1. "Guilt is the fact or condition of having committed an offense, especially a willful violation of a legal or moral code" (*The Reader's Digest Great Encyclopedic Dictionary*)
     2. This willful violation of moral integrity brings deep feelings of remorse
  C. *Why You Feel Guilty and What to Do About It*

II. **Body**
  A. *You May Feel Guilty Because You* Are *Guilty*
     1. David felt guilty because of his sins (vv. 3–4)
     2. Let's admit that we are all guilty before God (Rom. 3:10–25)
     3. Like Belshazzar, we've been weighed and found wanting (Dan. 5:27)
     4. Guilt feelings can have a positive effect
        a. They are like the warning signs of cancer
        b. They are like pains that warn of a serious problem
        c. They may come from an awakened conscience
        d. They may result from the conviction of the Holy Spirit
     5. Thank God for guilt feelings if they bring you to Him
  B. *You May Feel Guilty Because You Have Not Been Forgiven*
     1. How David felt before confessing his sins and receiving forgiveness (vv. 3–4)
        a. He felt older than his years
        b. He felt as though God was against him
        c. He felt as though he was in a spiritual desert

211

    2. Forgiveness was available to David, but he had not accepted it

      a. The Lord's invitation to be forgiven (Isa. 1:16)

      b. The Lord's payment for our sins (Isa. 53:5–6)

      c. The Lord's guarantee of forgiveness (Heb. 7:25–28)

      d. Heaven's celebration of forgiveness (Rev. 5:9–10)

    3. Our forgiveness depends on accepting God's gracious offer to sinners

    4. Even grace does not force forgiveness on us

C. *You Can Be Free from Guilt by Accepting Forgiveness*

    1. David finally sought and found forgiveness (v. 5)

      a. Read and identify with the guilty king's confession (Ps. 51)

      b. David's confession of his sins fits us all

    2. Sins confessed are sins forgiven

      a. "thou forgavest the iniquity of my sins"

      b. This will always be true (1 John 1:9)

III. Conclusion

    A. *Why Remain a Prisoner of Past Sins?*

    B. *Bring Your Sins to the One Who Died for Sinners*

    C. *You Don't Have to Feel Guilty Anymore*

Book Burning

Acts 19:18–20

I. **Introduction**
   A. *Ephesus: The Third Capital of Christianity*
      1. Jerusalem . . . Antioch . . . Ephesus
      2. A large city noted for being the location of the temple of Diana
         a. The most magnificent building in Asia Minor
         b. A center of sorcery and superstition
   B. *Paul's Powerful Ministry in Ephesus*
      1. His longest stay in any city—two years—was in Ephesus
      2. He spent three months ministering in the synagogue, then he formed a church
      3. The results were miracles, transformed lives, and many new believers
   C. *Why These New Believers Burned Their Books*

II. **Body**
   A. *Book Burning Revealed Their Personal Faith in Christ (v. 18)*
      1. Many Ephesians believed and confessed their faith openly
      2. Those who had been involved in sorcery burned their books
      3. These books had meant a lot to them before their conversion
         a. They considered these books to be sacred sources of guidance
         b. They had turned to them during times of trouble
         c. They looked upon these books as the tools of astrologists and psychics
      4. Now these believers would look to Christ for guidance
      5. They wanted to burn their bridges behind them, depending completely on Jesus
   B. *Book Burning Became Their Public Testimony for Christ (v. 19)*
      1. They burned their books "before all men"

2. Public book burning testified of their faith in Christ
   a. Flames reaching upward declared, "We trust Jesus."
   b. Some people shrink from public identification with Christ
   c. Some people want salvation's blessings but not its reproach
   d. Some people hide their light instead of letting it burn in the night
3. Some people refuse to be baptized and shun church membership
4. Christ was baptized and crucified publicly
5. We should seize opportunities to witness boldly for Him

C. *Book Burning Revealed the Value They Placed on Jesus (v. 19)*
1. "They counted the price"
   a. These books were worth fifty thousand pieces of silver
   b. Judas betrayed Jesus for thirty pieces of silver
   c. What's your price?
2. These book burners loved Jesus more than their possessions
3. They wanted everyone to know that Jesus came first in their lives
   a. They were completely committed to Him
   b. He came first whatever the cost

III. Conclusion
  A. *Consider the Cost of Calvary's Cross*
  B. *How Will You Respond to Such Love?*
  C. *What Keeps You from Surrendering Everything to Him?*

By All Means

1 Corinthians 9:22

I. Introduction
A. *The Mission of the Church Is Missions*
 1. We need to get excited about missions
 2. We need to renew our missionary vision
 3. We need to increase our missionary zeal and involvement
B. *Paul Was History's Greatest Missionary*
 1. Paul's goal in missionary work was to save some
 2. Paul was willing to identify with everyone to accomplish his goal
 3. Paul used all means of witness at his disposal and so should we

II. Body
A. *What "By All Means" Meant to Paul*
 1. It meant preaching in public places
  a. In synagogues and city squares
  b. In friendly and hostile settings
 2. It meant testifying boldly to individuals
  a. To prison inmates and the Philippian jailer (Acts 16:25–34)
  b. To Felix, the judge who wanted "a more convenient season" (Acts 24:25)
  c. To King Agrippa, who was almost persuaded but lost (Acts 26:28)
 3. Most of us are too timid to use all of the available means of witness
  a. We are slow to identify with people who are different from us
  b. Let's break down all barriers to save some
B. *What "By All Means" Means to Your Pastor and Missionaries*
 1. It means doing missionary work all of the time
 2. It means being aware of the present and eternal needs of lost people
 3. It means seeing people as God sees them
 4. It means sowing continually

       a. Giving out tracts and speaking to people about Christ

       b. Watching for and seizing special openings to tell of God's love

       c. Being alert for signs that people are hurting and open to receive a witness

    5. It means reaping whenever possible

       a. Presenting the gospel in love

       b. Sensing the work of the Holy Spirit

       c. Leading people to Christ

  C. *What Does "By All Means" Mean to You?*

    1. What are you doing to keep sinners from going to hell?

    2. Are you involved in witnessing in any way?

    3. Do you only sit and soak on Sunday, or are you seeking lost souls?

    4. Do you give out tracts? Share your testimony?

    5. Do you pray for souls to be saved as a result of your witnessing?

    6. How long has it been since you invited a lost person to church?

III. Conclusion

  A. *We All Meet Lost People Every Day*

  B. *Are We Concerned Enough to Use All Means to Reach Them?*

  C. *What Means Will You Use to Tell Someone of Jesus Today?*

Why Save Some?

1 Corinthians 9:22; Romans 3:23–25;
Matthew 11:28–30

I. **Introduction**
   A. *The Biblical Basis for Missions*
      1. "Go ye therefore and teach all nations" (Matt. 28:18)
      2. "Go ye into all the world, and preach the gospel to every creature" (Mark 16:15)
      3. "Ye shall be witnesses unto me" (Acts 1:8)
   B. *The Purpose of Missions: To Save Some*
      1. Paul's becoming all things to all people to save some
      2. Paul's using all means to save some
      3. Paul's goal of all missionary work: to save some
      4. Feeding and clothing goals should be to save some
      5. Housing and educating goals should be to save some
   C. *Why Is It So Important to Save Some?*

II. **Body**
   A. *The Problem of Sin (Rom. 3:23)*
      1. "Sin" is the word we'd most like to avoid
      2. Sin is the problem that is common to all people
      3. Sin is the cause of other serious problems: sorrow, suffering, and death
         a. The reason for most regret
         b. The cause of all crime
         c. The primary reason for emotional and physical pain
      4. There is no remedy for sin apart from the gospel (Acts 4:12)
   B. *The Plan of Redemption (vv. 24–25)*
      1. God's plan of redemption was announced in Eden (Gen. 3:15)
      2. Job spoke of his redeemer while suffering in the ash pit (Job 19:25)
      3. Isaiah prophesied of redemption without cost (Isa. 52:3)

217

    4. Isaiah presented the wounded redeemer (Isa. 53)
    5. Peter pronounced redemption through the precious blood (1 Peter 1:18–20)
    6. The cross was no afterthought with God
       a. David's suffering Savior (Ps. 22)
       b. The Lamb slain from the foundation of the world (Rev. 13:8)
    7. Christ crucified and risen solves our problem of sin (Heb. 7:25)
    8. How can we neglect our part in sharing the message of redemption?
       a. God has given so much—His Son
       b. We ought to do our part in saving some

  C. *The Pleading of Christ (Matt. 11:28–30)*
    1. Jesus continually invited sinners to come to Him and be saved
       a. Rich but lost Zacchaeus up in the sycamore tree (Luke 19:1–10)
       b. The unhappy woman at the well (John 4)
       c. The Lord's invitation to all to be saved (John 6:37)
    2. Christ is still pleading with sinners
    3. Missionary work is pleading with sinners on His behalf (2 Cor. 5:20–21)

III. **Conclusion**
  A. *Are We Really Willing to Become All Things to All People?*
  B. *Are We Really Willing to Use All Means to Save Some?*

I Surrender All

Romans 12:1–2

I. **Introduction**
   A. *Today's Missing Word: Commitment*
      1. A lack of commitment to marriage: broken homes
      2. A lack of commitment to church: just Sunday morning Christians
      3. A lack of commitment to evangelism: few believers witness
   B. *Paul's Call to Surrender All .*
      1. Surrender your body
      2. Surrender your mind
      3. Surrender your will

II. **Body**
   A. *A Call to Surrender Your Body (v. 10)*
      1. The passion of Paul's call
         a. "I beseech you"
         b. Wuest: "I beg of you, please"
      2. The reasons for Paul's compassionate call
         a. "Therefore" refers to all that precedes it
         b. This call is to believers: "brethren"
         c. It is "by the mercies of God": love, grace, and salvation
      3. "Present your bodies a living sacrifice"
      4. Wuest: "The physical body of the believer, put at the disposal of God is holy."
      5. "Your reasonable service," the intelligent thing to do
   B. *A Call to Surrender Your Mind (v. 2)*
      1. "Be ye transformed by the renewing of your mind"
      2. So much competition today for our minds
         a. So much to read: books, periodicals, etc.
         b. So much to see: television, videos, and computers
         c. So much to learn: Daniel's prophesied knowledge explosion
      3. How do we renew our minds?
         a. By tuning out negative information

219

      b. By spending time being quiet before God
      c. By developing a consistent devotional life
      d. By focusing on Bible promises and rejoicing in them
      e. By attending church regularly so that the Bible teaching brings spiritual growth

  C. *A Call to Surrender Your Will*
    1. "That good, and acceptable, and perfect will of God"
    2. Our stubborn wills crave satisfaction in the world (1 John 2:15–17)
      a. Bent on pleasure (the lust of the flesh)
      b. Bent on possessions (the lust of the eyes)
      c. Bent on self-exaltation (the pride of life)
    3. The world and its lusts are passing away
    4. Satisfaction comes when the will is surrendered to God

III. Conclusion
  A. *How Strong Is Your Commitment to Christ?*
  B. *Are You Willing to Surrender All to Him?*

Scripture Index